# W.R.I.T.E. R.I.C.H.™ Workbook:
# The Skill That Pays

Bridget K. Lambright-Tommelleo, M.Ed.

W.R.I.T.E. R.I.C.H.™

Copyright © 2025 by Bridget K. Lambright-Tommelleo

All rights reserved. No part of this publication may be reproduced, distributed, or transmitted in any form or by any means, including photocopying, recording, or other electronic or mechanical methods, without the prior written permission of the publisher, except in the case of brief quotations embodied in critical reviews and certain other noncommercial uses permitted by copyright law. For permission requests, email the publisher, at info@maximizeschool.com
www.maximizeschool.com

Ordering Information:
Quantity sales. Special discounts are available on quantity purchases by schools, corporations, associations, and others. For details, contact the publisher at the website above.
Printed in the United States of America
ISBN: 978-0-9796578-7-0

# W.R.I.T.E. R.I.C.H.™

## Table of Contents

Introduction .................................................................................. v
Just a Few Testimonials (I Have Hundreds) .......................... viii
Chapter 1: Good Credit = Credibility ....................................... 1
Chapter 2: Stack Your Message ................................................ 7
Chapter 3: Crisp Bills, Clean Bars ........................................... 12
Chapter 4: Upgrade Your Vocabulary Bank ......................... 17
Chapter 5: Titles and Hooks Get You Booked ...................... 23
Chapter 6: Don't Come Empty-Handed ................................ 28
Chapter 7: Punctuation Receipts ............................................ 34
Chapter 8: C.A.S.H.™ Paragraphs ........................................... 40
Chapter 9: Portfolio Stacking .................................................. 49
Bonus Chapter W.R.I.T.E. R.I.C.H.™ Method ........................ 55
Chapter 10: Style Is Money ...................................................... 61
Chapter 11: Credit Check Editing ........................................... 67
Chapter 12: The Writing Hustle .............................................. 73
Chapter 13: Prompt to Payday ................................................ 79
Chapter 14: Writing Wealth Habits ........................................ 86
Chapter 15: W.R.I.T.E. R.I.C.H. Mentorship Moves™ ........... 92
Chapter 16: Earn a Bonus Payment ........................................ 97
Chapter 17: W.R.I.T.E. R.I.C.H. Legacy Moves™ ................ 103
Epilogue ................................................................................... 110
My Plans Before My Paycheck .............................................. 113
W.R.I.T.E. R.I.C.H.™ Vocabulary Bank ................................ 118
W.R.I.T.E. R.I.C.H.™ Chapter Review Worksheets ............ 122
Special Thanks ........................................................................ 154
About the Author .................................................................... 155

W.R.I.T.E. R.I.C.H.™

*Gal, don't be common.*

- V. Melvin-Lambright aka Aunt Vi

## *Introduction*

Hello, I'm so glad that you're here. Let's keep it real. A lot of students grow up hearing you "don't write right." Teachers mark up your papers in red. People clown for "too much slang." Now, writing feels like a skill that only somebody else is good at.

W.R.I.T.E. R.I.C.H.™ flips that big lie on its ugly head. This method was built for students like you. Students with stories, style, and street smarts. Writing is money that's powerful, valuable, and worth stacking. Everyone deserves access to the money that good writing skills can bring. When you write well, people listen. Doors open. Cash flows.

I know because I've watched it happen hundreds of times to my former students in Cleveland, Ohio and Cleveland Heights, Ohio. Here's the truth. Every year, I met students who rolled their eyes, thought I talked crazy, or straight-up wished they had any teacher but me. Lots were salty because I wouldn't let them slide. I didn't give them A's like their other teachers. I pushed them harder than they'd ever been pushed. Sometimes too hard. But once their paragraphs started leveling up, they saw grades climb, and realized all the skills that their friends in other classes weren't being taught, they began to trust the process. Trust me.

Now, those same kids? They're grown. Some own businesses, some proudly wear military stripes, some flash college diplomas (first in the family!), and most of them earn really good money doing work they love. Yes, there are jobs where people are enjoying themselves so much that they love what they're doing while making great money. I'm talking $30, $40, $50, $60 and higher per hour! They travel the world, mentor others, raise successful kids, live wherever they want, and, best of all, move through rooms they never could have imagined at thirteen, fourteen, fifteen, sixteen, or seventeen years old.

They graduated from Harvard University, The Ohio State University, Howard University, The University of Akron, FAMU, Cuyahoga Community College, John Carroll University, Tennessee State University, Youngstown State University, Cleveland State University, and many other great trade schools or colleges. I could, but I'm not bragging. I'm simply sharing my receipts. I've got nothing to prove and zero reason to lie. I'm here because I love watching young people, especially those who have lots of people looking down on where they come from, win big.

My point? Writing = Wealth. Just like dollars, your words carry value: Pennies & Coins = common, overused words that don't buy much attention **versus** Bills & Benjamins = vivid, specific words that turn heads **versus** Pure Gold = phrases so sharp and clear they leave readers speechless. Even tough teachers become generous with A's. Stack the right words → craft smart sentences → invest in tight paragraphs, and you build a bank account of influence.

W.R.I.T.E. R.I.C.H.™ isn't just vibes. It's backed by research: Vocabulary Power = the bigger your word bank, the further you go in school, careers, and paychecks. Self-Belief = when you know your words matter, confidence floods in and excuses run out. Money Talk = everybody understands cash even if you don't have stacks yet. Turning "money moves" into "writing moves" makes learning click.

W.R.I.T.E. R.I.C.H.™ won't erase your voice. This method makes it impossible to ignore. Own your story, organize your thoughts, and express your power so you can cash in at school and in life.

Are you ready to get rich with your words? Let's go.

W.R.I.T.E. R.I.C.H.™

## *Just a Few Testimonials (I Have Hundreds)*

*Because of Ms. Lambright, I was able to get ahead in school and take college courses. Her expectations were that you would be the best. There was no maybe.*

- Chardonay Brown, MA, LPCC-S

*Everything we did in Ms. Lambright's class was to prepare us for college because to her it was not about if we were going to college as much as it was about when we went to college.*

- Martale, PhD from Kent State University

*Mrs. Lambright-Tommelleo is a phenomenal educator whose passion for excellence and student empowerment is unmatched.*

- Dr. Kennie Green, APS Program Manager

*We, urban students, face adversities that shrink our interest in education and overshadow the benefits of being academically inclined. Bridget provides a set of practical readiness skills that will not only spark your interest in education, but prompt you to reap its many benefits. These tips are the difference between getting a job and establishing a career or* **making cash and making money***!*

- Deonte, BA from Youngstown State University

*Ms. Lambright had the attitude of a hardcore realist who took no excuses. She stood by the philosophy to break the chain of poverty and enslaved poverty thinking by becoming better than our environment. She was bold enough to shed light on the ignorance of our generation.*

- Lavyisha, BA from Tuskegee University,
MA from University of Memphis

*If you want to reduce some of the anxiety related to the first day, week, month or year of college then read the book and apply the tips!*

- Rhonnetta, BSSW & MSW from The Ohio State University

**W.R.I.T.E. R.I.C.H.™**

*You always had us look in directions we didn't know was possible.*

> - Chanel, BA from The Ohio State University,
> MBA from University of Phoenix

W.R.I.T.E. R.I.C.H.™

# CHAPTER 1
# GOOD CREDIT
### CREDIBILITY IS KEEPING YOUR WORD.

Do you know what it means to have good credit? I'm not talking about school credit or extra points on an assignment. I'm talking about real life credit. The kind that helps grown-ups and even some teens buy cars, move into the fancy apartment or house they want, or swipe a credit card at the store and pay later. That's credit: someone gives you something now because they trust that you'll pay it back later.

Let me break it down for you in student terms. Say you're in the lunchroom and you forgot your lunch money. The lunch lady says, "It's okay, you can eat today and pay me Friday." That's credit. But here's the deal, if you keep your word and pay her back on Friday, she'll probably trust you again next time. You've got good credit. Now imagine someone else forgets their

1

lunch money too, but they never pay the lunch lady back. After a while, she's gonna stop helping. Why? Because that kid now has bad credit. Their word doesn't mean much.

That's the same way credit works when you grow up. Honestly, it starts now. Your credit is your reputation. It's how much people can count on you. That's what companies, landlords, and even schools look at when deciding whether to give you opportunities. And guess what? Writing works the same way.

*Your Writing Credit = Your Credibility*

When you turn in sloppy work, don't finish your sentences, or throw together words without effort, it's like not paying the lunch lady back. You start building bad credit as a writer. People stop listening. Teachers stop being flexible. Readers stop caring. But if your writing is thoughtful, clear, and organized (even if it's not perfect), people will start to trust your voice. You earn credibility. That means folks take you seriously. They respect your message.

Over the years, I've had hundreds of students who didn't believe me at first. They didn't like me. The majority even hated having me as their teacher. I pushed them hard. Made them follow specific rules. Challenged them when they wanted to give up. Refused to accept goofy mistakes. But once they got better, once they saw the power of their own words, they started trusting the process. Now? They're out here winning. Lots of them have certifications or college degrees. Some own businesses. Some are in the military, earning medals, and moving up the ranks.

Like I said before, almost all of them are making really good money, as well as living lives they couldn't have dreamed of because of their age or where they came from.   They were too young or stuck in one city to know what they didn't know. Now, almost a thousand of them are my Facebook friends. Every day, I get to see them winning regardless of how tough some of their lives started. I want to help you win, too. So, before we even get into how writing is like stacking cash, let's talk about how to keep your writing credit clean. I've had these rules for almost thirty years. They are guaranteed to get you paid in full. And I'm about to share them with you. Use them.  Respect them. They'll keep you from bankrupting (ruining) your message.

Please, pay attention. Your glow-up starts now.

# W.R.I.T.E. R.I.C.H.™ CREDIBILITY CHECKLIST

*Keep your writing credit clean. Get taken seriously.*

If you want your writing to earn respect, not just grades, check your work against this list before turning it in. Don't mess up your writing credit. Fix these first.

## 1. Do I have a full message, not just random thoughts?

✓ Did I stay on topic the whole time?
✓ Did I make a point, tell a story, or answer the question?

Sloppy thoughts = bad credit.
A focused message = good credit.

## 2. Did I use real sentences (not run-ons or fragments)?

✓ Can I tell where one sentence ends and the next begins?
✓ Did I avoid "text talk" like "bc," "u," or "idk" unless I'm writing dialogue?

Broken sentences are like a check that will bounce. Don't send them out.

## 3. Did I use powerful words (not just the same tired ones)?

✓ Did I upgrade weak words like "good," "stuff," "thing," and "said"?
✓ Did I try a $10 or $20 word that matches my message?

W.R.I.T.E. R.I.C.H.™

The more valuable your words, the more respect you earn.

## 4. Did I give enough information to back up my point?
✓ Did I give examples, reasons, or descriptions?
✓ Did I write at least 5–10 words in my sentences?
✓ Did I write at least 6–10 sentences in my paragraphs?

If you're asking for respect, don't give them pennies. Bring the full stack.

## 5. Did I use punctuation that makes my writing easy to follow?
✓ Do I have periods, commas, and capital letters in the right places?
✓ Did I check for quotation marks if someone is speaking?

Your punctuation is your receipt because it shows the reader you paid attention.

## 6. Did I read it out loud to catch mistakes?
✓ Does it sound like me but smarter?
✓ Did I catch anything weird or confusing when I read it out loud?

If it sounds messy, it probably is. Clean it up.

### 🧠 7. Did I put in effort or just rush through it?
✓ Would I be proud to show this to someone who matters to me?
✓ Did I rewrite or fix anything I know could be better?

Lazy writing = bad credit.
Effort shows you're worth investing in.

### 👑 Bonus: Did I write like someone who deserves a seat at the table?
✓ Does this writing show my intelligence, creativity, or growth?
✓ Will this writing build my reputation or break it?

Your words are your brand. Make them count.

### 📝 Final Tip: Before you turn it in, ask:
✓ Would I give ME a loan if this writing was my application?
✓ If not, go back and rewrite. Protect your credit.

## BRIEF EXPLANATION

Money never just "shows up" in your bank account. You plan for it, stack it, and track it. Your writing works the same way. Your teacher gives you a writing prompt, test question, or essay topic. If you care about your grades or have dreams of earning lots of money in a few years, then you're going to start planning your response. How you feel about the assignment or teacher doesn't matter. If you care about money, then you're just focused on completing every activity to practice, get feedback, and keep improving. So, it all starts with your ideas. The better your ideas, the more money you're setting yourself up to earn. Adults who have more money than you can imagine forced themselves to learn money-making skills at your age. Like amazing athletes, the earlier you start, the more time you're giving yourself to get really good. In this chapter, you'll learn how to budget your ideas, spend them wisely, and walk away with writing that's paid-in-full.

W.R.I.T.E. R.I.C.H.™

# STORY TIME

### *Aaliyah & the Sneaker Raffle*

Aaliyah (7th grade) wanted the new Jordan 5s that dropped at midnight. Ticket price: $150. She had only $60 saved but four weeks left. The first week, she hustled: babysitting, selling snacks, and cleaning. Every dollar went in a jar. Week two, she dipped into the jar for fast food, TikTok merch, and an Uber she didn't need. By Friday, her balance was $38. She learned fast: random spending = no Js. So, she set a budget, labeled envelopes ("babysitting," "snacks," "savings"), and quit impulse buys. On drop day, she walked in with $155 cash.

Writing works the same way. Start with one goal (a clear message) and protect it from distractions and impulse tangents. Stick to the plan, and you'll "cop" the grade, the respect, and the opportunities.

W.R.I.T.E. R.I.C.H.™

# REAL TALK & HOW TO

*The B.U.D.G.E.T. Method™ for a Paid-in-Full Message*

| Steps | What it means | Money Move | Writing Move |
|---|---|---|---|
| **B**rainstorm | List every idea fast | Empty pockets onto the table | Jot bullets with no judging yet |
| **U**nify | Circle the main idea | Choose the biggest bill | Pick ONE clear purpose |
| **D**ivide | Group related points | Sort bills & coins | Create 2-4 buckets (paragraphs) |
| **G**uard | Cross out off-topic stuff | Block impulse buys | Slash anything that drifts |
| **E**xpand | Add details & examples | Invest for growth | Explain, describe, prove |
| **T**ally | Read start-to-finish | Count your cash | Check flow & adjust order |

💡 **Pro Tip:**
If a sentence can't be traced back to your ONE big idea in two steps or less, it's an overdraft fee that will put you in the negative. It's time to delete or rewrite it.

## THE SKILL THAT PAYS

- Focused writing shows teachers, coaches, and scholarship committees that you respect their time.
- Cash Value: Good grades lead to good scholarships. Your future bosses will pay for your clear ideas.

## CHALLENGE YOURSELF

1. Pick a Topic: "Best way to spend a free Saturday in my city."
2. Apply the B.U.D.G.E.T. Method™.
3. Keep it to one page, three paragraphs.
4. Swap papers with a classmate/friend and highlight any sentence that feels off-topic in yellow.
5. Revise until zero yellow remains.

## SELF-CHECK

- Which step in B.U.D.G.E.T. do you skip the most and why?
- How does that same habit show up when you handle real money?
- What's one change you'll make this week to tighten both your wallet and your writing?

## FINANCIAL ADVICE

Plan your words like your dollars. Every sentence is on purpose and every paragraph is for profit.

We'll level up each sentence so your ideas flow like direct deposit into your bank account.

# BRIEF EXPLANATION

A dollar bill only spends if it's whole. Rip it in half or tape three together sloppily, and the cashier looks at you funny. Sentences work the same way. A run-on is like shoving two crumpled bills together and calling it a twenty. A fragment is that ripped corner nobody wants. This chapter shows you how to keep your sentences crisp, complete, and ready to cash.

# STORY TIME

## *Jalen & the Endless Text*

Jalen (6th grade) wrote the hottest sneaker blog in class, except his sentences never stopped. One post read: "These Red Octobers are fire they dropped at midnight everybody in the city wants a pair but the price is wild if you stack your money you might grab them but hurry before bots eat them all." Great ideas, but it felt like sprinting down the block without breathing. His readers got lost (and tired). After we chopped the paragraph into clean sentences, his views doubled. Lesson: Give readers room to breathe or they bounce just like money out of a holey pocket.

# REAL TALK & HOW TO

*The B.I.L.L.$.™ Sentence Stack*

| Steps | What it means | Money Move | Writing Move |
|---|---|---|---|
| **B**reathe | Pause at natural breaks | Count each bill, not the wad | Read your draft out loud, mark where you gasp |
| **I**solate | Find one idea per sentence | One purchase = one receipt | Ask, "What is this line really about?" |
| **L**ink | Connect ideas the right way | Use a money clip, not duct tape | Add a period + capital or a comma + conjunction (and, but, so) |
| **L**ength-Check | Keep sentences wallet-sized | A $100 bill fits neatly, a yard of pennies doesn't | Aim for 8–20 words; anything over 25, break it |

| $ubstance | Swap weak verbs/words | Upgrade pennies to quarters | Trade "is/are" for action verbs, replace "good" with "outstanding," "massive," etc. |

> 💡 **Pro Tip:**
> - Run-On? Split with a period or add "and/but/so."
> - Fragment? Add the missing subject or verb.
> - Double-check capital letters after every period. No lowercase counterfeits allowed.

## THE SKILL THAT PAYS

- Currency: Clear sentences get you better grades, cleaner raps, and sharper IG captions.
- Respect Points: Adults skim, so they trust writers who hit hard and quit rambling.
- Payday Later: Job apps & scholarship essays with run-ons hit the trash. Crisp sentences land interviews.

W.R.I.T.E. R.I.C.H.™

## CHALLENGE YOURSELF

1. Grab last week's B.U.D.G.E.T. paragraph.
2. Highlight run-ons in red and fragments in blue.
3. Use B.I.L.L.$.™ to fix each.
4. Trade papers, and a partner signs off only if every sentence is whole.

## SELF-CHECK

- Which step in B.I.L.L.$.™ feels toughest: breathing, isolating, linking, length-checking, or upgrading?
- How does that struggle show up when you handle real money (impulse buys, messy wallet, etc.)?
- One sentence habit you'll change this week.

## FINANCIAL ADVICE

Break your words like bills. Create one crisp idea at a time instead of loose change in a lump.

# NEXT UP

We're going to learn how to stop paying with loose change like "stuff," "things," and "good." Now is the time to start stacking your writing with $10, $20, even $100 words that earn real attention. The richer your words, the richer your message. Let's go upgrade your writing account to stay paid-in-full, fam.

## BRIEF EXPLANATION

If every word you use was a type of money, what kind of spender would you be? Some people stay broke because they only use pennies: basic, boring words like "good," "bad," "stuff," "thing." Other people walk in with $50 and $100 bills. They use vivid, powerful words that make readers *feel* a certain emotion. Let's help you upgrade your writing with rich words that make people pay attention.

## STORY TIME

### Destiny & the Word Switch

Destiny (8th grade) was writing about her grandma's cooking. Her first sentence? "My grandma's food is good." I stopped her and said, "That sounds like it came from a vending machine." She laughed. I asked, "What kind of good?"

She thought for a second and rewrote it: "My grandma's food hugs your insides like a warm blanket after school."

Now we're talking! I could taste it. Her one-dollar word ("good") just turned into a whole deposit of flavor and feeling. That's the power of using better words. You get more reaction, more respect, and more credit.

# REAL TALK & HOW TO

*The W.O.R.T.H.™ System for Word Value*

| Steps | What it means | Money Move | Writing Move |
|---|---|---|---|
| **W**atch Out for Weak Words | "Good," "bad," "stuff," "thing," "nice," etc. | These are pennies. Cheap and everywhere. | Circle them when you revise. Replace them. |
| **O**pen a Word Bank | Collect high-value words from music, books, and convo | Like saving up for a big purchase | Start a "Rich Word Vault" in your notebook |
| **R**ate Word Value | Ask: Does this word paint a picture or leave it blank? | $1 vs. $100 word | Example: "mad" → "furious" or "boiling" |
| **T**est the Tone | Pick words that match the vibe you're aiming for | Don't bring a gold chain to a job interview | Write for your audience: keep it real but on point |
| **H**ustle with Verbs | Verbs are action money and they move the reader | Weak verb: "is"/ Rich verb: "shatters," | Find the *one verb* that does the heavy lifting |

|  |  | "slams," "builds" |  |

## Common Word Upgrades

| $1 Weak Word | Richer Options |
|---|---|
| good | flavorful, amazing, unforgettable, powerful |
| bad | toxic, unfair, dangerous, frustrating |
| said | whispered, shouted, argued, admitted |
| went | stormed, wandered, dashed, drifted |
| thing, anything, something, nothing, everything | device, memory, habit, moment |

> 💡 Pro Tip:
> Don't just sound smarter. Be more specific. Rich words = rich meaning = rich pockets

# THE SKILL THAT PAYS

- Reader Respect: People take you more seriously when your words hit hard.
- Job-Ready: Employers notice clear, sharp writing, especially with action words.

- Scholarships & Essays: Power words = power moves. Judges don't reward boring.

## CHALLENGE YOURSELF

1. Pick five weak words you overuse (check your past writing).
2. Write each one in a notebook.
3. Come up with at least three replacements for each.
4. Rewrite an old paragraph using the new words.

## SELF-CHECK

- Which weak word do you run to when you're stuck?
- How does that compare to spending small in real life when you could invest bigger?
- What's a $100 word you learned lately that you're proud of?

## FINANCIAL ADVICE

The richer your words, the bigger your impact. Don't talk like you're broke.

# NEXT UP

You've started stacking your Vocabulary Bank to trade-in weak pennies for power words that make your writing pop. But even rich words need a strong place to live. We're building the paragraph like it's real estate. We're talking structure, flow, and purpose = the C.A.S.H.™ Paragraph system.

W.R.I.T.E. R.I.C.H.™

## BRIEF EXPLANATION

When you're scrolling through YouTube, TikTok, or Netflix, what makes you click? A title that grabs you. A thumbnail that pops. In writing, your hook and title do the same thing. They stop readers in their tracks. Whether it's a teacher grading papers or a real-world audience reading your letter, blog, essay, application, or article, the first impression matters. That's why you've got to make your introductory sentence and title earn you money.

## STORY TIME

### Brittany and the Mad Click

Brittany was heated. She slammed her Chromebook and said, "I don't even care anymore. I did all that writing. She gave me a C because my title was weak? Really?!" Yup. Really.

Brittany wrote a beautiful story about taking care of her little brother when her family was homeless. It had emotion, action, and even a twist. But the title? It said: "My Story." And her hook? "This story is about me being a good big sister." The reader (her teacher) didn't feel intrigued. It felt like clicking a video that said "Bad Stuff Happens." Brittany's message got buried under basic packaging. After rewriting her title to "I Dug Deep to  Pull Myself Out," and starting with, "This world may be full of quitters, but I was born a winner." The opening reminded Brittany of every night she went to bed hungry and cold. Her same teacher reread it, gave it an A, and read it out loud to the class. She even asked Brittany to give a presentation for a group of homeless parents. Brittany felt like someone had just given her $1,000. That's how much your title and hook matter.

W.R.I.T.E. R.I.C.H.™

# REAL TALK & HOW TO

*H.O.O.K.$. Formula™*

| Steps | What it means | Money Move | Writing Move |
|---|---|---|---|
| **H**ighlight the Heat | Start with something bold, dramatic, or urgent | Headline-grabbing = attention paid | Banned Book Gets a Standing Ovation |
| **O**ffer a Big Idea | Blow your reader's mind | Drop knowledge, not questions | Jail is worth fighting for justice… |
| **O**wn the Emotion | Tap into curiosity, anger, pride, or humor | Feelings make it personal and profitable | I refused to stay silent… |
| **K**eep Titles Short | Make it tight and punchy | Quick hits = quick grabs | Crushed But Always Clawing and Climbing |
| **$**ell It Like a Brand | Make it catchy, clever, unforgettable | Hooks = hype = high value | Confessions of a Class Clown or The $5 Haircut That Changed My Life |

> 💡 **Pro Tip:**
> Don't give it all away. Just like a movie trailer, your hook should tease the best part. Use a remix or get inspired like a scholar.

## THE SKILL THAT PAYS

- Standout: You'll stand out to teachers, judges, readers, and anyone deciding whether to take you seriously. That's real value.

## CHALLENGE YOURSELF

1. Take your last three writing assignments and rewrite the title and hook using the H.O.O.K.$. Formula™. Share with a peer or adult and ask which one they'd click on.
2. Practice with song titles. Look at your favorite tracks and ask, "What makes this title pop?"

## SELF-CHECK

- Are my titles and hooks basic, boring, or forgettable? Do they give people a reason to read or a reason to skip?

## FINANCIAL ADVICE

If your hook doesn't pull, your pay won't pop.

## NEXT UP

Anybody can *say* whatever they want. But in the next chapter, we're going to talk about proving it. Writing without support is like showing up to buy shoes with no money. Nobody's buying what you're selling. You'll learn how to back up your ideas with evidence, examples, and explanations that make your words undeniable. It's time to show the receipts.

## BRIEF EXPLANATION

Let's say you walk into the mall and see a pair of $180 Jordans. You walk up to the counter with the box in your hand, and the cashier says, "Alright, let me ring you up." You reach in your pocket and pull out nothing but lint and confidence. No wallet. No cash. No card. No ID. Nothing. You'd probably hear, "Uhh… where's your money?" and be escorted right back to the racks. That's what happens when you make a big claim in your writing but don't back it up with anything. No examples. No evidence. No explanation. You came to the reader empty-handed. Expect them to buy what you're selling, but you brought no proof to pay for it. In writing and in real life, you can't expect people to believe you if you can't show them the receipt. Your credibility takes a hit when you drop strong opinions but leave your paper looking like an empty wallet.

# W.R.I.T.E. R.I.C.H.™

This chapter is about teaching you how to show up fully loaded. Bring real-life examples, detailed stories, specific moments, and clear reasons that make your message undeniable. If you're gonna make a point, do it like a boss. Pull out your writing wallet and slap a stack of receipts on the table.

## STORY TIME

### *Manuel & the Hall Pass Lie*

Manuel (11th grade) got caught in the hallway with no pass. When the assistant principal stopped him and asked what he was doing, Manuel said: "My teacher told me to come down here." That's it. No name. No time. No paper. No context. Just one sentence. You think they believed him? Not a chance. Later that day, when things calmed down, Manuel explained again, but this time with receipts: "Ms. Johnson told me to take this form to the office. She gave it to me after our warm-up at 9:10 because I finished the quiz early."

Now, that? That's detail. That's backup. That's bringing proof to the table. Writing works the exact same way. A statement with no explanation is like saying, "Trust me," while holding out empty hands. But when you show up with examples, reasons, and details? That's how you earn credit and keep it.

# REAL TALK & HOW TO

*The R.E.C.E.I.P.T.™ Formula: Proof That Pays Off*

| Steps | What it means | Money Move | Writing Move |
|---|---|---|---|
| **R**eal Example | Tell a real or believable situation | You brought the actual item | Use a moment from your life, a story, or a common situation your reader will connect with |
| **E**vidence | Give a fact, stat, quote, or source | Proof of purchase | Add information that shows your idea is legit. What did you read, observe, or hear? |
| **C**onnect It | Link the example to your main point | Swipe the card that makes it go through | Explain how the story proves what you're saying |
| **E**xplanation | Break it down in your own words | Count the change | Don't assume the reader "gets it" and |

**W.R.I.T.E. R.I.C.H.**™

|  |  |  | spell it out with confidence |
|---|---|---|---|
| **I**nclude Details | Add names, time, setting, and feelings | An itemized receipt | Be specific about who, where, when, what, why, and how |
| **P**aint a Picture | Help the reader visualize it | Full-color ad, not a black-and-white receipt | Use sensory language: how did it feel, smell, sound? |
| **T**ie it Back | Bring it home to your main idea | Bag it up and carry it out | End the paragraph by clearly stating what we should believe now |

💡 **Pro Tip:**
Strong claims need strong support. When you back up your ideas with clear examples, explanations, or evidence, you don't just sound smarter. You prove you've got the writing credit to be taken seriously.

# THE SKILL THAT PAYS

- School: More proof = better grades and fewer red marks.
- Street: Even your homies won't believe you if your story keeps switching.
- Success: In interviews, speeches, or debates, support makes you unforgettable.

# CHALLENGE YOURSELF

1. Pick one:
    a. "Why my neighborhood needs more places for teens"
    b. "Why I deserve more freedom at home"

2. Now apply R.E.C.E.I.P.T.™:
    ✓ Real example
    ✓ Evidence
    ✓ Connection
    ✓ Explanation
    ✓ Details
    ✓ Visuals
    ✓ Wrap-up sentence

3. Next: Swap with a classmate and highlight each part. Missing a section? Write a rewrite.

## SELF-CHECK

- When have you said something true but people didn't believe you?
- What proof did you leave out that would've helped?
- What do you need to start bringing to your writing so nobody can doubt you again?

## FINANCIAL ADVICE

A strong message with no receipts is just noise. Pay up with proof or leave it out.

## NEXT UP

We've got your message clear, your sentences clean, your word value high, and your proof stacked. But now, it's time to make it all official with the punctuation tools that show you know what you're doing. Let's talk about punctuation receipts.

W.R.I.T.E. R.I.C.H.™

## BRIEF EXPLANATION

When you shop, the cashier hands you a receipt. That receipt shows **what you bought**, **when you bought it**, and **how much you paid**. It's proof you handled your business. Now, imagine someone tries to return shoes with no receipt. They claim they bought them, but the manager says, "Nah, you can't prove that." Same with writing. You could have the strongest ideas in the world, but if your punctuation is wild, sloppy, or missing, your writing looks unprofessional. It reads like someone who's guessing, not someone who came prepared.

Punctuation is your receipt. It tells the reader you paid attention to details. Tiny marks = major meaning. When you leave them out, you leave your writing open to confusion, chaos, and comedy. Every period, comma, question mark, or quotation mark shows you knew what you were doing. In this chapter, we're going to turn boring punctuation rules into Money Moves that make sense and make your writing stronger, clearer, and cleaner.

# STORY TIME

## *Sammie's Text Message Mix-Up*

Sammie (8th grade) sent this text to her friend about a birthday party: "Let's eat grandma!" Her friend didn't respond. Later, her mom saw the text and said, "Why are you talking about eating Grandma?" Sammie was confused… until someone pointed out she forgot a **comma**. What she meant to say was: "Let's eat, Grandma!"

That tiny comma changed the message. Without it, it sounded like Grandma was on the menu. One little punctuation mark turned a sweet invite into a horror movie plot.

W.R.I.T.E. R.I.C.H.™

# REAL TALK & HOW TO

*The R.E.C.E.I.P.T.S.™ Guide to Punctuation Power*

| Steps | What it means | Money Move | Writing Move |
|---|---|---|---|
| **R**ecord = Periods (.) | Ends a full thought | Final price stamp | A period "records" the end of a transaction |
| **E**numerate = Commas (,) | Pauses and separates | Price tags on items | Commas list or count items |
| **C**larify = Question Marks (?) | Shows you're asking | Asking the price before buying | A question mark asks for clarity |
| **E**mphasize = Exclamation Marks (!) | Adds emotion or energy | Tip added to the receipt | Exclamations add urgency |
| **I**ndicate = Quotation Marks (" ") | Shows what someone said | Receipt comments or feedback | Shows someone's exact words |
| **P**rovide = Parentheses ( ) | Add extra info quietly | Discounts listed in small print | Provides side info or discounts |

| **T**ie Together = Colons (:) & Semicolons (;) | Introduce or separate related items | Splitting bills or pairing items on a receipt | Link related info clearly |
|---|---|---|---|
| **S**how Ownership = Apostrophes (') | Show ownership or missing letters | Receipt belongs to YOU | Show who or what something belongs to |

💡 **Pro Tip:**
Think of punctuation like respectful spacing in a text conversation. If you send one long message with no stops, people get overwhelmed or confused.

## THE SKILL THAT PAYS

- Credibility: People read clean writing and assume you're smart, organized, and serious.
- Clarity: Punctuation helps the reader understand exactly what you're really saying without any guessing.
- Communication: Whether it's a blog, a scholarship essay, a rap, or a business email, your punctuation is your tone.

# CHALLENGE YOURSELF

1. Pick a paragraph you've already written.
2. Use the R.E.C.E.I.P.T.S.™ chart to check each punctuation type.

3. Use a color-coded system:
   - Red = periods
   - Blue = commas
   - Green = quotation marks
   - Orange = question marks/exclamation marks
4. Make sure at least **five different punctuation types** are included.
5. Fix any word that's missing, overused, or confusing.

# SELF-CHECK

- Do I have a period at the end of every full sentence?
- Did I pause where a reader might need a breath (commas)?
- Did I use punctuation to match my tone? Did I overdo it or underdo it?
- Could someone read my writing and understand my voice?

# FINANCIAL ADVICE

The more detailed your receipt, the more professional you look. A sloppy receipt makes people think you don't care or you're lying. Punctuation is the difference between looking rich and being rich in skill.

W.R.I.T.E. R.I.C.H.™

## NEXT UP

You've built a powerful message, written it with style, backed it up with proof, and now you've stamped it with punctuation. But structure matters too. Let's take your paragraph game to the next level with C.A.S.H.™ Paragraphs. Learn how to stack your ideas so every point flows like payday. Let's go.

## BRIEF EXPLANATION

Think back to everything you've banked so far:

| Skill | Money Move | Why It Matters |
|---|---|---|
| B.U.D.G.E.T.™ = Full Message | Drew up a spending plan | No impulse buys, no wasted ideas |
| B.I.L.L.$.™ = Clean Sentences | Kept bills crisp & un-creased | Readers trust you and read on |
| Vocabulary Bank = Rich Words | Swapped pennies for Benjamins | Your writing sounds valuable |
| R.E.C.E.I.P.T.™ = Proof | Flashed the receipt | No one can doubt your claim |
| Punctuation Receipts | Itemized every detail | Looks professional, feels legit |

Those chapters were your financial boot camp teaching you to earn (ideas), save (sentence control), invest (word choice), verify (evidence), and document (punctuation). Now it's time for the paycheck: one powerful paragraph that rolls all that effort into a neat, spendable stack. A paycheck doesn't trickle in as random coins. It lands as a single deposit you can use right away. The

# W.R.I.T.E. R.I.C.H.™

C.A.S.H.™ Paragraph Method does the same for your writing. It bundles your claim, evidence, explanation, and mic-drop closer into one tight unit that hits your reader's mental bank account in seconds.

Why should you care? Because:
- Teachers grade faster than TikTok scrolls. C.A.S.H.™ gets them nodding "A" before they finish line two.
- Employers skim a hundred cover letters. C.A.S.H.™ makes yours the one that gets the call-back.
- Influencers, activists, entrepreneurs, or anyone trying to change minds or chase the bag can't afford messy paragraphs. C.A.S.H.™ turns your message into money-making clarity.

## STORY TIME

### *Carlos & the Chaotic DM*

Carlos (8th grade) wanted to convince a sneaker reseller to lower a price on limited-edition kicks. He DM'd: "Yo, price too high, I had these before, I'm loyal, been wanting them, let me get a deal." Zero structure. The reseller left him on read. So, Carlos tried again using C.A.S.H.™:

**Claim:** "I'm offering $180 today for the Smoke Grey 1s."

**Assets:** "Check my profile. Twenty legit buys, five-star feedback."

**Spending:** "I can pay through Cash App or meet at SneakerCon this Saturday."

**Hook-back:** "Deal with me now and you clear inventory before the next drop."

Result? The seller replied in ten minutes: "Bet. $180 works. See you Saturday." His structure sealed the deal.

# REAL TALK & HOW TO

*Option A: The C.A.S.H.™ Blueprint*

| Steps | What it means | Money Move | Writing Move |
|---|---|---|---|
| **C**laim | A one-sentence statement of your main point | Your paycheck stub headline | One clear sentence stating your main point |
| **A**ssets | Evidence, examples, or reasons that support your claim | Proof of funds | 2-3 sentences of evidence, examples, or reasons |
| **S**pending | Explaining how or why your evidence matters | Where the money goes | 2–3 sentences of explaining how or why your evidence matters |
| **H**ook-back | Wraps it up and returns to your claim | Closing the vault | 2–3 sentences tying everything back to your Claim + strong finish |

Example Paragraph (Topic: School Lunch Needs an Upgrade)

**C = Claim:** Our school cafeteria needs healthier, tastier lunch options.

**A = Assets:** Last month's student survey shows 72 % throw away veggies and the nurse reported a spike in afternoon sugar crashes.

**S = Spending:** Adding fresh fruit bars and grilled-chicken wraps would cut waste, boost energy, and keep students focused for seventh-period math. Harder subjects like Math require more attention. The brain cannot function properly without sufficient nutrition.

**H = Hook-back:** Investing in better meals now pays off in stronger grades and fewer nurse visits. Kids depend on adults to create positive learning environments. Food selection is just as important as the other resources that administrators purchase for students. Good health equals good profit for the whole school.

W.R.I.T.E. R.I.C.H.™

*Option B: The D.E.P.O.S.I.T.™ Slip*

| Steps | What it means | Money Move | Writing Move |
|---|---|---|---|
| **D**rop the Topic Sentence | Start strong with your main idea | State the purpose up front | Write a clear topic sentence that tells readers what the paragraph is about |
| **E**xplain the Idea | Add insight to your claim | Break it down for the reader | Clarify what your topic means and why it matters |
| **P**rovide Evidence | Show the receipts | Back it up | Use examples, facts, quotes, or observations that support your point |
| **O**ffer Analysis | Count the change | Explain the value of the evidence | Describe how your evidence connects to your claim |
| **S**hare More Support | Stack the bills | Build wealth in the paragraph | Add another example or reason to |

|  |  |  | deepen the argument |
|---|---|---|---|
| **I**nclude Transitions | Keep the cash flowing | Smooth and steady | Use words or phrases to link ideas clearly |
| **T**ie It Back | Seal the vault | Lock it in | End with a sentence that restates or reinforces the main idea |

💡 **Pro Tip:**
You've practiced every move. Now use them all at once and cash out big.

## THE SKILL THAT PAYS

- Academic Cash-Out: Essays, short-answer tests, and prompts score higher.
- Career Currency: Bosses love clear structure in applications, emails, cover letters, presentations, etc.
- Street Value: Persuade parents, coaches, or community leaders when you need support.

# CHALLENGE YOURSELF

1. Pick a topic you care about (school changes, neighborhood upgrades, phone rules in class, etc.).
2. Draft one C.A.S.H.™ paragraph.
3. Swap with a classmate. Each of you label C, A, S, and H in the other's work.
4. If any letter is missing or weak, revise until the bag is full.

# SELF-CHECK

- Claim: Can someone read my first sentence and know my point?
- Assets: Did I show receipts using facts, examples, stats?
- Spending: Did I explain how my Assets prove the Claim?
- Hook-back: Did I loop back to the Claim with a punch?
- Did every earlier skill (rich words, clean sentences, punctuation) stay on point?

# FINANCIAL ADVICE

A paragraph without C.A.S.H.™ is like a paycheck with deductions you didn't approve. Putting in lots of work for a little reward would be a nightmare. Use C.A.S.H.™ and watch your writing income rise.

# NEXT UP

C.A.S.H.™ locks down the paragraph, but an essay is a portfolio with multiple paychecks growing together. Next, we'll master portfolio stacking: linking paragraphs so your whole essay compounds like interest on a high-yield savings account. Get ready to multiply your money words!

W.R.I.T.E. R.I.C.H.™

## BRIEF EXPLANATION

Let's get real: one paragraph is cool, but it's just one paycheck. If you're trying to build wealth, one check won't cut it. You need a system. A stream. A portfolio. A source that keeps paying you overtime. In writing, that means learning how to stack multiple paragraphs to build a full essay—each one holding weight, working together, and pushing your message higher. This isn't just about writing more, it's about writing smarter so your paragraphs support each other instead of just sitting there like strangers in the same room.

Remember:
- **B.U.D.G.E.T.™** helped you organize your message.
- **C.A.S.H.™** taught you how to build one powerful paragraph.

Now you're going to link paragraphs like blocks in a building that are solid, smooth, and built to last. You might be writing an argument essay for school, a speech to run for student council, a post for your blog, a complaint about an adult, or even a caption that needs to carry weight. Whatever it is, you'll need a structure that **holds up under pressure**.

Portfolio Stacking is that structure. This is how smart writers turn one good idea into a success story that earns them A's, awards, scholarships, opportunities, and even dollars. No lie. This chapter will teach you how to turn your C.A.S.H.™ into a whole writing investment plan so you're not just making a point; you're building an empire.

## STORY TIME

### Jada's Essay Win

Jada (12th grade) entered an essay contest for a local nonprofit. The winner got $250 and their piece printed in the city newspaper. Her first draft? A fire opening paragraph and then four weak ones that rambled, repeated the same ideas, or went off track. Her teacher said, "Each paragraph should be a new deposit and not the same coins reshuffled." So, Jada rebuilt using Portfolio Stacking:

- One strong **intro paragraph** with her clear claim.
- 3-4 **body paragraphs** and each with its own C.A.S.H.™.
- One **conclusion paragraph** that tied it all together.

She won first place. That essay is still framed on her grandma's wall.

W.R.I.T.E. R.I.C.H.™

# REAL TALK & HOW TO

*The P.A.I.D.™ Strategy for Stacking Paragraphs*

| Steps | What it means | Money Move | Writing Move |
|---|---|---|---|
| **P**lan Your Stack | Use an outline to organize your ideas | Don't blow the check on one bill | Know how many paragraphs you need and what each one's job is |
| **A**lign Your Paragraphs | Keep all your writing focused on one central point | Keep all deposits in the same bank | Make sure each paragraph supports the same main idea or claim |
| **I**nvest in Transitions | Create smooth flow between ideas | Link your checks into a steady stream | Use transition words/phrases to connect ideas smoothly |
| **D**ouble-Down in the Conclusion | Reinforce your message and leave a strong final impression | Reinvest the earnings | Restate your main idea in a fresh way and leave a lasting thought or call to action |

W.R.I.T.E. R.I.C.H.™

> 💡 Pro Tip:
> Don't waste space in your essay with off-topic or repeated ideas. If it doesn't **grow the main point**, it doesn't belong. Strong outlines help your writing stay focused, rich, and worth reading.

Example Essay (Topic: "Why My School Should Start Later")
- Intro: Clear claim = Students need more sleep.
- Body 1: Health benefits = backed with R.E.C.E.I.P.T.™.
- Body 2: Academic performance increases.
- Body 3: Safer commute with less rushing.
- Conclusion: All students' grades, health, safety would win. Let's put kids first by changing the start time.

## THE SKILL THAT PAYS

- Grades Go Up: Teachers give higher scores to organized essays that build strong points over time.
- Real-Life Ready: Resumes, applications, speeches all rely on clear, connected structure.
- Respect Grows: Adults take you seriously when you sound like you thought it through. You're a joke to them when you repeat yourself.

W.R.I.T.E. R.I.C.H.™

# CHALLENGE YOURSELF

1. Pick a topic:
    a. Social media can be good for teens.
    b. School uniforms should/shouldn't be required.
    c. The best way to spend $1,000 on your community.
2. Create a plan with P.A.I.D.™:
    a. One intro
    b. Three body paragraphs (use C.A.S.H.™)
    c. One conclusion
3. Use transition phrases between each paragraph:
    a. First of all, On the other hand, For example, As a result, Most importantly, Finally, In conclusion
4. Have a classmate check that your stack is complete and doesn't have any missing links.

# SELF-CHECK

- Does each paragraph have its own purpose and proof?
- Did I use transitions to guide the reader through my thoughts?
- Is my conclusion strong enough to stand on its own like the final line in a rap?
- Would I be proud to submit this whole stack as a final draft?

## FINANCIAL ADVICE

One paycheck feeds you today. A portfolio feeds you for life. Stack your paragraphs like you're stacking assets. Each one valuable, working together, and growing your worth.

## NEXT UP

During the last nine chapters, you've been leveling up. Now's a good time to show you the big picture before you stack even more skills. This bonus chapter is where I tied it all together for my former students. If I could go back in time, I would've gone skill-by-skill like how I'm showing you in this workbook.

You're learning the full W.R.I.T.E. R.I.C.H.™ method, step by step, so your writing hits harder, earns more, and stands out for real.

W.R.I.T.E. R.I.C.H.™

## BRIEF EXPLANATION

Hello! You've covered a lot so far. Before you start the second half of this workbook, I've included a commercial break. You're probably wondering about what W.R.I.T.E. R.I.C.H.™ stands for. This chart shows how real writers make money moves on paper. Every lesson in this book connects to these W.R.I.T.E. R.I.C.H.™ skills. Think of it like your blueprint. Your cheat code. Your money map.

## STORY TIME

### *Nay Knew She Was Ready*

Nay had already gotten into college. That part was done. But now she was required to attend a three-week camp called a Summer Bridge Program before the fall semester started. On day one, she looked around the room. Most of the kids looked like her.

She thought it was interesting. Nay asked one of the counselors, "Where is everyone else and why are we here?" The counselor didn't sugarcoat it. He replied, "This program is for students from urban districts. New students in this group have the highest dropout rate. The college is trying to fix that by getting y'all stronger before fall." Nay just nodded. She didn't feel offended. She felt motivated. She had already been training for this moment.

That very first day, the dean came in, introduced herself, and scribbled a prompt on the board. She said, "You have forty minutes. Show us your writing level." Most of the other students looked around like this woman was crazy. Many grumbled, "We need more info! What are we supposed to say? This prompt is too random!" But Nay didn't flinch. She opened her notebook and went to work. Eight really good paragraphs later, she handed in her pages and walked out of the room like she had just dropped a hit record. The next morning, her name was called. She had tested out of Freshman English. When they returned her paper, the feedback read: "What school district did you attend? Were you privately schooled?"

Nay smiled. Nope. Public school. Urban district. But trained in the W.R.I.T.E. R.I.C.H.™ method since 9th grade. She stayed in touch with her high school crew, and like her, they all tested out of Freshman English. That moment told her everything she needed to know. She was built for this. Her writing training wasn't just about high school grades—it gave her the power to show up and show out when it mattered most.

# REAL TALK & HOW TO

*W.R.I.T.E. R.I.C.H.™: The Writer's Investment Plan*

| Steps | What it means | Money Move | Writing Move |
|---|---|---|---|
| **W**ords Have Worth | Every word counts | Choose words like you're spending cash | Use precise, meaningful vocabulary |
| **R**espect the Rules | Follow the grammar game like banking rules | Grammar = trust in the writing world | Structure, grammar, and punctuation matter |
| **I**nvest in Ideas | Build something valuable with your thoughts | Don't just write, build value | Use strong claims, themes, or thesis statements |
| **T**rack Your Thinking | Keep receipts of your process | Proof of thought = proof of funds | Use examples, explanations, and logic |
| **E**dit Like It's Expensive | Polish your work like it's going on display | Don't waste your final product | Revise and polish every draft |

W.R.I.T.E. R.I.C.H.™

| **R**ead Like You Want to Get Paid | Read smart to write smart | Smart readers earn more | Study mentor texts, directions, and examples to write with purpose and swag |
|---|---|---|---|
| **I**nclude Receipts | Show your proof | Proof earns respect | Back up ideas with evidence, facts, quotes, stats, examples, or details |
| **C**onnect with the Reader | Write like it matters to someone | No buyer? No sale | Know your audience. Make them care. |
| **H**ustle for High-Quality Writing | Push to improve | More effort = more earnings | Never assume that your reader is convinced |

💡 **Pro Tip:**
When someone reads your writing, they're spending their time and energy on you instead of doing other activities. Time is money. Don't leave them broke. Pay them back with solid skills so they walk away feeling like the time they gave you was worth it.

W.R.I.T.E. R.I.C.H.™

## THE SKILL THAT PAYS

- Prompt Mastery: Reading between the lines and writing with confidence sets you apart the moment you hit submit.
- College-Level Confidence: Knowing how to respond with structure, clarity, and voice gets you noticed and placed ahead of the pack.
- Response Power: When others freeze, you deliver. That kind of power opens doors most students never reach.

## CHALLENGE YOURSELF

1. Set the scene. Imagine it's day one of college. Your professor writes this quote on the board: "Success doesn't happen by accident." Then says: "You've got thirty minutes. Respond with at least four to five paragraphs."
2. Start the clock. Grab your notebook or device. Set a timer for thirty minutes. No complaints. No excuses. Write like this moment counts.
3. Go all in. Use the W.R.I.T.E. R.I.C.H.™ Method: organize your ideas, hit every paragraph with a hook, back up your points, and keep your sentences sharp.

4. Check yourself. Read your writing out loud. Does it sound like a college-level writer? Would someone celebrate or mock the school that taught you how to Write?

## SELF-CHECK

- Can I answer a writing prompt clearly without needing extra help or time?
- Do my ideas flow in paragraphs with strong support and details?
- Can I explain, prove, and back up my point like a pro?
- Am I confident enough in my writing to skip freshman English?

W.R.I.T.E. R.I.C.H.™

## BRIEF EXPLANATION

Let's be honest: there's a difference between having money and having money with style. You ever seen someone with a basic outfit but the *way* they wear it? Fire. Or someone with average sneakers, but the laces, the walk, and the confidence—it's a whole look. That's what style does. It turns regular into memorable. In writing, style is your drip, your fingerprint, your flavor. It's how you say what you say. Do you sound confident? Clear? Too stiff? Too sloppy? Boring? Bold? Dry like saltines or spicy like Hot Cheetos?

Your style can either break your writing or make people lean in and want more. But here's the thing: style doesn't mean breaking every grammar rule just to sound "cool." Nah. It's about balance and knowing how to bring your *personality* into your writing while keeping your clarity, purpose, and C.A.S.H.™ structure strong.

If writing is money, then **style is branding:**
- It's what makes people remember you.

# W.R.I.T.E. R.I.C.H.™

- It's what makes your message stand out in a stack of essays.
- And when you get it right? It's like walking into a room and everyone knowing exactly who you are even before you speak.

## STORY TIME

### *Trey's Boring Bio*

Trey (8th grade) was asked to write a short bio for his music program's website. Here's what he turned in: "My name is Trey. I'm fourteen years old. I like music. I'm excited to perform." Yawn. That's not a bio. That's the instruction manual for a cheap toothbrush. We asked him to **add some style.** Keep it true but let his voice shine.

His second try: "I'm Trey, fourteen, future Grammy-winner, and beat-maker since my cousin showed me how to sample at age ten. If it's got rhythm, I'll find the flow. Music isn't just what I do, it's how I breathe. Can't wait to rock this stage."

Now, that? That's writing with money and swag. He kept it clean, confident, clear, and still fully him.

# REAL TALK & HOW TO

*The F.L.A.V.O.R.™ Formula for Writing Style*

| Steps | What it means | Money Move | Writing Move |
|---|---|---|---|
| **F**ind Your Tone | Your voice is your brand | Your style is part of your brand | Are you serious, funny, emotional, or bold? Pick the tone that fits your purpose |
| **L**evel Up Your Word Choice | Designer words over bargain bin | Vocabulary is your outfit | Swap plain words for vivid ones that match your message (see Vocabulary Bank) |
| **A**dd Personal Touches | Custom fit over generic | Make your writing one-of-a-kind | Share your slang, experience, or humor without losing clarity |

W.R.I.T.E. R.I.C.H.™

| **V**ary Sentence Lengths | Mix of big bills and coins | Keep it flowing like cash | Short punchy lines + longer expressive ones = rhythm |
|---|---|---|---|
| **O**wn Your Grammar | Wear the rules like a tailored suit | Flex like a pro | Break a rule on purpose, not by accident—know the difference |
| **R**ead It Out Loud | Test the fit before you wear it out | Check the price tag | If it sounds boring or fake, rewrite it until it feels like you |

💡 Pro Tip:
Style is what keeps a reader engaged **after** they've understood what you're saying. It's the reason they remember you.

## THE SKILL THAT PAYS

- Personal Essays Pop: Admissions and scholarship readers love unique voices
- Brands Pay for Style: Social media writers, content creators, and influencers make money with words that "feel real"

- Authenticity Builds Trust: When your writing feels like you (not a copy-paste student), you stand out

## CHALLENGE YOURSELF

1. Pick a boring paragraph you wrote earlier. Use the F.L.A.V.O.R.™ Formula to remix it.
    a. Add rhythm.
    b. Swap tired words.
    c. Throw in a line that sounds exactly like you.
2. Bonus Round: Read both versions aloud to a partner. Which one hits harder?

## SELF-CHECK

- Did I stay on topic but still bring me into it?
- Did my word choice give personality without sounding sloppy?
- Did my paragraph still follow the C.A.S.H.™ format while showing my voice?
- Could someone hear my tone and *see* my vibe in the writing?

W.R.I.T.E. R.I.C.H.™

## FINANCIAL ADVICE

You can have money, but if you don't have style, you won't get invited to the next level. In writing and in life, presentation pays. When presentation pays, your work's looks matter just as much as what it says. If your writing is messy or rushed, people might not even notice the smart stuff inside. When it's clean, clear, and put together, you earn more respect, more points, and more chances to shine. Make sure yours is dressed to earn.

## NEXT UP

You've got ideas, flow, proof, structure, and you've added style. Self-editing is next. Even the richest writing needs cleaning before it's cashed. Credit Check Editing™ is about how to fix mistakes that mess up your writing credit and make your message bounce like a bad check. Time to polish. Let's run that credit report.

**W.R.I.T.E. R.I.C.H.™**

## BRIEF EXPLANATION

Let's say you applied for a job or apartment and the person in charge ran your credit report. If your score is low, your bills are unpaid, or you've got a bunch of errors on your record, guess what? You get denied even if you're actually good for it. Writing is no different. You can have a great idea, solid proof, and rich vocabulary, but if your final product is messy, sloppy, or full of careless mistakes, people stop trusting your message. You lose writing credit. Think of editing like checking your writing bank statement before you turn it in. You're making sure nothing is missing, no "charges" were accidental, and the whole assignment reflects your true value.

You've already:
- Built a full message (**B.U.D.G.E.T.™**)
- Cleaned your sentences (**B.I.L.L.$.™**)
- Upgraded your word choice (**W.O.R.T.H.™**)
- Tightened up you titles and hooks (**H.O.O.K.$™**)
- Brought receipts (**R.E.C.E.I.P.T.™**)

- Used punctuation like a pro (**R.E.C.E.I.P.T.S.™**)
- Structured your paragraphs (**C.A.S.H.™ and D.E.P.O.S.I.T™**)
- Stacked them into essays (**PA.I.D™**)
- And added your unique voice (**F.L.A.V.O.R.™**)

Now it's time to review the whole transaction to make sure it's tight, clean, and cashable. Only writing that's edited earns top dollar.

## STORY TIME

### Amira's Almost-A Essay

Amira (7th grade) turned in her best essay yet. Fire claim. Great structure. Real examples. But when the teacher handed it back, it said B+. Why not an A? The comments said. "Too many little mistakes: typos, missing capitals, run-ons. You're too smart for this kind of sloppiness." Amira hadn't reviewed it. She rushed the final step. When she edited and resubmitted for a second chance, her grade went up.

Moral of the story? **Smart ideas don't shine if they're covered in mess.** I've been saying since I first started teaching how bad writing is like bad breath.

W.R.I.T.E. R.I.C.H.™

One burns the eyes, the other burns the nose. Clean up your draft like it's your rep on the line.

# REAL TALK & HOW TO

*The C.R.E.D.I.T.™ Checklist for Editing Like a Boss*

| Steps | What it means | Money Move | Writing Move |
|---|---|---|---|
| **C**apitalization | Big names need a capital to show respect | Respect your title like a paycheck stub | Proper nouns, sentence starters, and "I" are always capitalized |
| **R**un-Ons & Fragments | Don't mash coins together or leave change out | Separate bills correctly | Use punctuation to break up full thoughts and fix incomplete ones |
| **E**rrors in Spelling | Misspelling is like fake bills, they get rejected | Spell check is like counterfeit detection | Double-check tricky words, use tools but don't rely |

|  |  |  | only on autocorrect |
|---|---|---|---|
| **D**ouble Words/Missing Words | Like charging someone twice or not enough | Accurate billing matters | Read aloud to catch repeated or dropped words |
| **I**nconsistent Tone | Don't switch currency mid-deal | Use one consistent currency | Make sure your tone stays formal, passionate, or personal throughout |
| **T**idy Formatting | Presentation = professionalism | Neatness = value | Indent paragraphs, space correctly, and use consistent font if typed |

💡 **Pro Tip:**
Read your work out loud. Your ear catches what your eye skips.

W.R.I.T.E. R.I.C.H.™

# THE SKILL THAT PAYS

- A+ Ready: Teachers grade faster when they see clean, polished work.
- Professional Level: Employers and scholarship panels don't excuse sloppy work. Clean writing shows respect and readiness.
- Confidence Boost: When you edit your own work, you own it. You stop guessing and start growing.

# CHALLENGE YOURSELF

1. Grab your latest essay or paragraph.
2. Run a full C.R.E.D.I.T.™ Check:
    a. Circle capitals
    b. Highlight punctuation issues
    c. Underline spelling fixes
    d. Mark repeated or missing words
    e. Put stars next to tone shifts
    f. Clean up formatting
3. Make all the changes, then rewrite or retype the final version.

Bonus Round: Read both versions to a peer. Ask: "Which version sounds richer, smarter, cleaner?"

## SELF-CHECK

- Did I fix errors that could embarrass me?
- Does my writing look like it came from someone who cares?
- Could I turn this in to a boss, coach, or admissions team with confidence?
- Did I do a final read-through or just hope it was good enough?

## FINANCIAL ADVICE

You don't hand over a wrinkled, ripped bill at the bank and expect full value. Same with writing. Clean it up or it won't cash out.

## NEXT UP

You've got credit-worthy writing now, but there's one more level: getting paid in real life. The Writing Hustle™ is how to use all these skills for scholarships, money moves, resumes, college apps, competitions, and real-world opportunities. Because rich writing should lead to real returns. Let's get you to the bag.

W.R.I.T.E. R.I.C.H.™

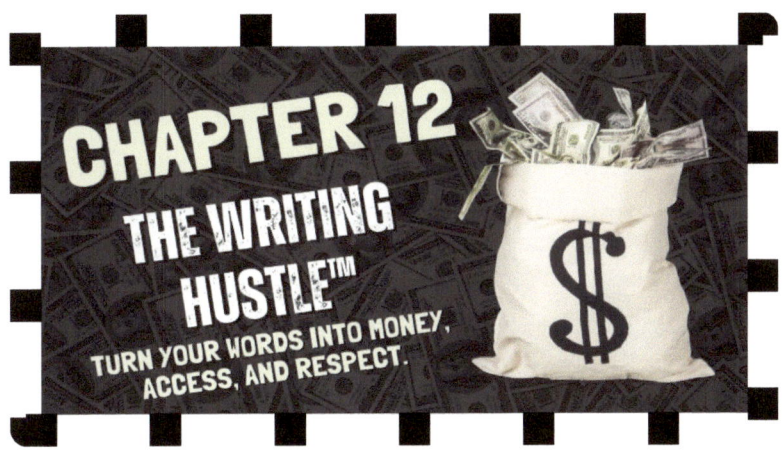

## BRIEF EXPLANATION

You've been stacking skills this whole time. You've learned to:

✓ Budget your message
✓ Build crisp sentences
✓ Use richer words
✓ Bring receipts
✓ Add punctuation with purpose
✓ Structure paragraphs with C.A.S.H.™
✓ Stack essays like a portfolio
✓ Add your unique F.L.A.V.O.R.™
✓ Run that final credit check

That's not just writing; that's writing wealth. Now it's time to flip your writing into real-life profit: grades, scholarships, leadership roles, internships, cash prizes, and other bag-securing opportunities. This chapter is all about the Writing Hustle™ and how to use your skills not just for school but to elevate your life.

W.R.I.T.E. R.I.C.H.™

Here's the truth: Students who can write well get chosen more often, paid more quickly, and trusted more deeply.

Whether you're applying for an opportunity/money, persuading someone, standing out in a crowd, or making your voice heard, writing is the hustle that pays quietly but deeply. The world isn't looking for perfect grammar. It's looking for people who can **communicate clearly, confidently, and convincingly**. You already have the toolbox. Now let's learn to use it *on purpose*.

## STORY TIME

### *Devin Gets the Grant*

Devin (10th grade) heard about a $1,000 youth entrepreneur grant. He had a great idea: to make and sell custom beaded wristbands with inspirational words like "Focus," "Hustle," and "Respect." He almost didn't apply because he didn't think he could write a proposal. Then he remembered everything he learned in W.R.I.T.E. R.I.C.H.™:

- He used B.U.D.G.E.T.™ to plan his message
- He wrote a C.A.S.H.™ paragraph for his pitch
- He added real examples with R.E.C.E.I.P.T.™
- He used style with F.L.A.V.O.R.™
- And he edited with C.R.E.D.I.T.™ like a boss

# W.R.I.T.E. R.I.C.H.™

His writing wasn't just strong—it was undeniable. He won the grant, bought supplies, and started his business. And when he got his first online sale? That money felt different. Because it came from his words.

## REAL TALK & HOW TO

*The H.U.S.T.L.E.™ Method for Writing That Wins*

| Steps | What it means | Money Move | Writing Move |
|---|---|---|---|
| **H**ighlight What You Bring | Know your worth | Show off your starting balance | Start by showing your strengths, skills, or personal story |
| **U**nderstand Your Audience | Pitch to the right investor | Know who's signing the check | Think: "Who's reading this? What do they care about?" |
| **S**how Evidence | Receipts earn trust | Back up your claim | Use examples, facts, or past wins to |

W.R.I.T.E. R.I.C.H.™

|  |  |  | support your message |
|---|---|---|---|
| **T**alk with Confidence | Speak like you've already earned it | Bold tone = higher offer | Avoid weak language like "I think," "I believe," "In my opinion," or "maybe" |
| **L**ead with Structure | Organized money moves faster | Build like a business plan | Use the C.A.S.H.™ Blueprint or full essay layout to stay focused |
| **E**nd with Impact | Don't just exit, close the deal like a boss | Final pitch that seals the deal | End strong with a call to action, a bold takeaway, or a reminder of value |

💡 Use this for:
- Scholarship essays
- Class speeches
- Grant proposals
- Business pitches
- Leadership applications
- Personal statements

- Even social media posts that need to be taken seriously

## THE SKILL THAT PAYS

- Money Moves: Grants, scholarships, and business contests are yours for the taking.
- Power Plays: Writing well earns you leadership roles, shoutouts, and trust from adults.
- Networking Game: A strong email or post can open doors you didn't even knock on yet.

## CHALLENGE YOURSELF

1. Choose one:
    a. Write a 1-paragraph pitch for a product, club, or cause you care about.
    b. Write a personal statement for a future job or scholarship.
    c. Write a "Why I Deserve This Opportunity" letter.
2. Use H.U.S.T.L.E.™ to guide the structure. Ask a peer: "Would this make you pick me over someone else?" If not, rewrite until it would.

## SELF-CHECK

- Did I clearly show why I deserve the opportunity?
- Did I organize my thoughts using my W.R.I.T.E. R.I.C.H.™ tools?
- Did I use real-life examples to prove I'm ready?
- Would this make someone want to invest in me?

## FINANCIAL ADVICE

Write like your future depends on it, because sometimes, it does. The bag doesn't always go to the loudest voice. It often goes to the clearest one.

## NEXT UP

You've now got the full writing hustle. If you want to stay paid, your writing habits must match your writing talent. Coming next is Writing Wealth Habits™. We'll look at how to build the discipline, mindset, and routines that keep your writing rich and your confidence growing. This is where skill turns into lifestyle. Let's build your writing legacy.

W.R.I.T.E. R.I.C.H.™

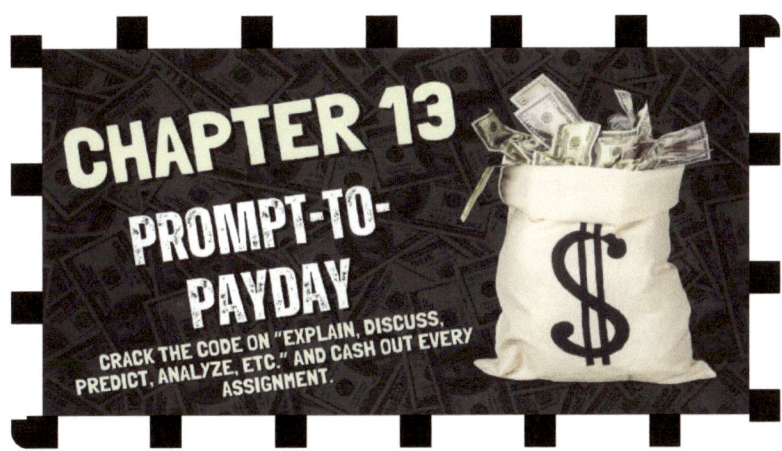

## BRIEF EXPLANATION

Ever freeze up when a teacher drops words like explain, analyze, justify in the prompt? You're not alone. Those verbs are like different payment methods at the store (cash, card, Apple Pay, etc.). If you swipe the wrong way, the transaction gets declined. This chapter is your translation guide. We'll decode the most common prompt verbs, what they really ask for, how much "writing money" you gotta put down, and a starter sentence stem to get you moving. Think of it as the difference between showing up with exact change versus digging around for coins while the line gets mad behind you.

You already learned the C.A.S.H.™, F.L.A.V.O.R.™, and H.U.S.T.L.E.™ moves. Now, you'll know how to choose the right *combo* the moment you read a prompt so you can answer fast, clear, and rich.

# STORY TIME

## *Leila's Lost Points*

Leila (9th grade) crushed her research, used big vocab, and cited sources. The prompt said "Predict how climate change may affect our city in twenty years." She wrote eight paragraphs explaining what climate change is but never made any predictions. Sadly, Leila had great info with the wrong credit card. Grade? C-. Next time, she checked the verb first, used a prediction stem ("In the next two decades, our city will likely … because …") and scored an A.

Moral: Match the verb to secure the bag.

W.R.I.T.E. R.I.C.H.™

# REAL TALK & HOW TO

*The P.A.Y. D.A.Y.™ Prompt Decoder Chart*

| Steps | What it means | Money Move | Writing Move |
|---|---|---|---|
| **P**ay Attention to the Prompt | Read the contract before the deal | Read with purpose | Highlight key words like explain, analyze, predict, etc. Know what it's asking. |
| **A**sk: What is it really asking me to do? | Break the job down before the hustle | Clarify your role | Rephrase the prompt in your own words to aim your answer right. |
| **Y**our Job is to Plan | You don't get paid without a plan | Organize the pitch | Map out ideas before writing. Choose your main point and how to back it up. |
| **D**ecide the Point of View | Choose the right voice for the job | Speak from the right account | Use 1st, 2nd, or 3rd person based |

|  |  |  | on the prompt to hit the right tone. |
|---|---|---|---|
| **A**nswer Every Part | Don't leave money on the table | Complete the invoice | Some prompts have multiple parts—answer each one fully. |
| **Y**ou Must Show the Proof | Receipts get respect | Provide verification | Use quotes, examples, or evidence to support your response. |

Here are some verbs that you can expect to see:

| Verb in Prompt | What It Really Means | Money Move | Starter Sentence Stem |
|---|---|---|---|
| Explain | Break it down step-by-step | Pay in small bills | "First… next… finally…" |
| Discuss | Give both sides/ major points | Split the check | "One important point is… however…" |
| Predict | Say what will happen & why | Invest in futures | "In the next ___, it's likely |

# W.R.I.T.E. R.I.C.H.™

|  |  |  |  |
|---|---|---|---|
|  |  |  | that… because…" |
| **Analyze** | Take it apart and show how the pieces work | Appraise the value | "A key part of __ is… which shows…" |
| **Identify** | Point out & name | Quick tap with Apple Pay | "The main __ is…" |
| **Justify** | Prove it's right with evidence | Show your receipt | "This is the best option because the data shows…" |
| **Persuade** | Change someone's mind | Make a sales pitch | "You should __ because…" |
| **Compare** | Show similarities & differences | Count stacks side-by-side | "Both __ and __ share… yet they differ in…" |
| **Summarize** | Give the short version, main points only | Deposit the essentials | "In short, __ happened because…" |
| **Evaluate** | Judge the value/give a rating | Price check | "Overall, __ is effective because… but…" |

💡 **Pro Tip:**
Highlight or circle the verb first, choose the correct stem or create your own starter, then plug in your C.A.S.H.™ evidence.

# THE SKILL THAT PAYS

- Test Time Beast: You answer exactly what the rubric wants without losing any points.
- Speed & Clarity: You spend less time staring at prompts and more time stacking high-value sentences.
- Confidence: Once you nail the verb, the rest flows like auto-deposit.

# CHALLENGE YOURSELF

1. Pick three verbs from the table.
2. Write one index-card answer (three to four sentences) for each using the starter stems.
3. Swap cards with a classmate. Do they match the verb's meaning? If not, revise until they do.

# SELF-CHECK

- Did I circle the prompt verb before writing?
- Did my first sentence match the correct stem?
- Did I include evidence or reasoning that fits the job (explain vs. justify, etc.)?
- Could my teacher read only my first two lines and know I understood the task?

## FINANCIAL ADVICE

Swipe the right card, the payment clears fast. Use the wrong one, and you're stuck at the register. Same in writing: match the verb, get paid in points and respect.

## NEXT UP

Now you can decode any prompt and respond like a pro. Time to build habits that keep this skill fresh and automatic. Writing Wealth Habits™ will suggest daily, weekly, and monthly routines that keep your writing credit sky-high and your future earning power limitless. Let's lock in the lifestyle.

## BRIEF EXPLANATION

You've come a long way. You didn't just learn to write; you learned to earn. You didn't just build paragraphs; you built value. You didn't just upgrade words; you upgraded your worth. But here's the truth: **Even millionaires go broke without discipline.** Having writing skills is only the beginning. Keeping it sharp, fast, and reliable takes practice. This chapter is about making your writing success a lifestyle.

I'm not talking about just a one-time test win or a lucky essay but a system that keeps you ready for any opportunity. At any moment. Whether that's a scholarship, contest, job app, resume, grant, class assignment, or college entry, you want your skills to be cash-on-hand ready. You don't need to write ten pages a day. You just need small, consistent habits that keep your writing credit score high and your confidence unshakable. This chapter is your blueprint for becoming writing rich for life.

W.R.I.T.E. R.I.C.H.™

# STORY TIME

## *Mason's Quick Win*

Mason (9th grade) wasn't top of the class, but he had one secret: a notebook in his backpack with three habits he never skipped:

- He wrote **3 new sentences every morning** using vocabulary from class, reading, or music.
- He did a 5-minute paragraph fix-it challenge twice a week.
- He kept a list of writing prompts and practiced one each Sunday night.

One day, a teacher said, "The class extra credit opportunity is to submit a persuasive letter by tomorrow." Most students panicked. Mason submitted his within an hour. It was clean, convincing, and C.A.S.H.™ strong. He didn't win by luck. He won because his writing stayed ready. That's what this chapter gives you: Readiness. Hustle. Habit. Wealth.

W.R.I.T.E. R.I.C.H.™

# REAL TALK & HOW TO

*The W.E.A.L.T.H.™ Routine: Writing Habits That Build Forever Skills*

| Steps | What it means | Money Move | Writing Move |
|---|---|---|---|
| **W**rite a Little Every Day | Daily deposits grow your savings | Small amounts add up | Spend 5–10 minutes a day writing: journal, captions, prompts, or story ideas |
| **E**dit Past Work | Reinvest and grow your returns | Improve what you already earned | Choose an old paragraph and apply the C.R.E.D.I.T.™ method weekly |
| **A**nalyze Good Writing | Study the millionaires | Learn from proven earners | Read songs, blogs, or essays and ask: "Why does this hit?" |

W.R.I.T.E. R.I.C.H.™

| **L**earn New Words Weekly | Grow your word bank | Build your vocabulary savings | Add 5–10 new words to your personal Vocabulary Bank each week |
| **T**rack Your Growth | Check your statement balance | Watch your wealth grow | Save old writing samples and compare monthly to see progress |
| **H**elp Someone Else Write | Spread the wealth | Share knowledge and lift others | Edit a friend's paragraph or teach them a tip you've learned |

💡 Pro Tip:
Don't try all six at once. Pick two to start and grow from there.

## THE SKILL THAT PAYS

- Consistency Wins: Talent fades without training, but habits keep you sharp.
- Opportunity Ready: Last-minute assignments? Scholarship due tonight? No sweat, you're already in shape.
- Leadership Energy: You become the one others ask for help, and that builds respect, confidence, and community.

## CHALLENGE YOURSELF

1. Create your personal W.E.A.L.T.H.™ Plan:
2. Choose three habits to start with.
3. Decide how often and when you'll do them.
4. Write them in a notebook or calendar.
5. Give your plan a title (ex: "My Pen Stays Paid Plan" or "Word Bank Builder").
6. Stick to it for thirty days and track your progress.

## SELF-CHECK

- Have I made writing part of my weekly routine, even if it's small?
- Do I review or reflect on my writing like it's worth money?
- Am I improving my vocabulary or sentence game consistently?

- Do I help others or lead writing moves in class or in my circle?

## FINANCIAL ADVICE

A big check is exciting, but a steady income builds power. Make writing part of your daily hustle and watch your opportunities multiply.

## NEXT UP

You've built the habits. Now, it's time to inspire others. WRITE RICH Mentorship Moves™ shows how to turn your writing wealth into leadership, peer support, and a legacy. The final level of success isn't just getting paid, it's helping others rise with you. Let's create writing leaders.

W.R.I.T.E. R.I.C.H.™

## BRIEF EXPLANATION

You've come all the way up:
- ✓ You understand prompts
- ✓ You write power paragraphs with C.A.S.H.™
- ✓ You use receipts to prove your point
- ✓ Your style is strong, your edits are clean, your essays are stacked
- ✓ You've even started building habits that keep your skills sharp

Now you're sitting on writing wealth. But here's the truth about real success. It's not just about keeping the bag. It's about helping others fill theirs too. This chapter is about turning your writing skills into mentorship power by helping classmates, younger students, or even your siblings level up. When you teach someone else, you get stronger too. People will look up to you. You become a leader, not just a learner.

Mentorship is a flex:

# W.R.I.T.E. R.I.C.H.™

- It shows confidence without arrogance
- It builds respect with adults and peers
- And it proves you don't just know the game, you can coach it

## STORY TIME

### *Jayda the Coach*

Jayda (11th grade) wasn't the loudest in class. But during peer review day, she helped three classmates fix their paragraphs using C.A.S.H.™ and R.E.C.E.I.P.T.™. One student said, "Nobody ever explained it like that before." The teacher pulled her aside and said, "You should lead the next workshop."

Later that year, Jayda was chosen to co-lead the student writing center and ended up getting invited to speak at a middle school writing camp. She didn't pull any flashy moves. She just offered what she knew, and people noticed.

# REAL TALK & HOW TO

*The G.I.V.E.™ Method for Being a WRITE RICH Mentor*

| Steps | What it means | Money Move | Writing Move |
|---|---|---|---|
| **G**uide, Don't Show Off | Teach them to earn, not borrow | Support, don't flex | Say: "Want me to help break it down?" instead of "Just copy me." |
| **I**dentify What They Need | Know what they're missing before you help | Ask before you act | "What part's confusing you?"/"Which section feels weak?" |
| **V**alidate Their Effort | Boost their writing credit score | Acknowledge growth | Celebrate wins like: "That example hit!" or "You fixed your run-ons, let's go!" |
| **E**xplain Using the Tools | Pass the blueprint, not just the results | Share strategies | Walk them through fixes using |

|  |  |  | B.U.D.G.E.T.™, C.A.S.H.™, etc. |
|--|--|--|--|
|  |  |  |  |

> 💡 **Pro Tip:**
> You don't need to be perfect to help someone; you just need to care enough to help them get better.

## THE SKILL THAT PAYS

- Leaders Are Noticed: Teachers, counselors, and coaches recommend students who help others.
- You Learn More by Teaching: Explaining a skill to someone else helps you master it.
- You Change the Culture: Your school, class, or friend group levels up and they start seeing writing as power, not punishment.

## CHALLENGE YOURSELF

1. Pick one person to mentor this week:
    a. A younger student, classmate who struggles, or friend who hates writing
    b. Ask if they want support
    c. Pick one W.R.I.T.E. R.I.C.H.™ tool to focus on (C.A.S.H., R.E.C.E.I.P.T., etc.)
    d. Spend 10–15 minutes walking them through their writing

e. Reflect: What did you teach them? What did you learn from teaching?
2. Bonus: Journal about how it felt to help someone else.

## SELF-CHECK

- Do I help without taking over or making others feel small?
- Do I use my W.R.I.T.E. R.I.C.H.™ tools when giving feedback?
- Have I grown more confident by helping others?
- Am I building a circle that's leveling up with me?

## FINANCIAL ADVICE

Mentors don't lose money. They multiply it. The more people you help build wealth (in writing, knowledge, or skill), the more valuable you become. That's how legacies are made.

## NEXT UP

Point of view controls who's telling the story. Now it's time to get sharp about which person to use: *1st, 2nd,* or *3rd.* Most students get this wrong, but not you. Knowing when to use "I," "you," or "they" can earn you more money, respect from readers and teachers, and result in clearer writing. In this next lesson, you'll learn how the right person makes your writing stand out and how the wrong one can cost you. Let's cash in on the power of person.

## BRIEF EXPLANATION

Want to earn bonus respect, higher grades, and extra opportunities? Learn how to flex your point of view like a pro. Most middle and high school students mess this up, but not you. Once you know when and how to use 1st, 2nd, or 3rd person correctly, your writing will stand out. Teachers, scholarship judges, and future bosses all notice this subtle skill and they reward it.

# STORY TIME

## *Don't Include Ms. Lambright*

Every single year, I had to remind students, "I haven't been in high school in over thirty years." Why? Because some of them would always write, "We all know how hard high school is…" or "In our school…" I had to let them know that I'm not in school with you. You just lost points. Don't include the reader unless you're told to. This happens all the time, and it's one of the fastest ways to mess up an otherwise good paper. But the students who learned this trick early? They started sounding like experts, not just students. Their work had an edge. It sounded stronger, smarter, and more professional.

W.R.I.T.E. R.I.C.H.™

# REAL TALK & HOW TO

*Person Pays: The Power of POV in Writing™*

| Steps | What it means | Money Move | Writing Move |
|---|---|---|---|
| **P**ick the Right Person | Choose the right account | Choosing the Right Account | Just like choosing the right bank account for your money, pick the best POV for the assignment. |
| **O**wn Your Purpose | Spend with intention | Spending with Intention | Know why you're writing: personal (1st), teaching (2nd), or storytelling/informational (3rd). |
| **V**oice That Fits Reader | Speak their currency | Speaking Their Currency | Match the POV to your reader: "I" for personal, "you" for direct, "they" for distant/professional. |

*When to Use Each POV*

| POV | Used For | Examples | Money Move |
|---|---|---|---|
| **1st Person** | Personal narratives, opinion pieces, reflections | I, me, my, we, us | Use only when you're asked to speak from your experience. |
| **2nd Person** | Instructions, directions, | You, your | Rare, but powerful |

|  | persuasive letters, "how-to" writing |  | when teaching or giving advice. If teachers or essay judges are reading, avoid using. |
| --- | --- | --- | --- |
| **3rd Person** | Formal essays, research, reports, storytelling, news | He, she, they, people, the student, them | Most academic and professional writing should use this. |

💡 **Pro Tip:**
As you get older and take on harder writing assignments, 1st person is used less and less. It sounds too casual and personal. In most academic writing, 2nd person can make your paper sound unprofessional. That's risky or rude. Third person gives your writing a level of trust and seriousness that stands out.

## THE SKILL THAT PAYS

- Task Recognition: Using the right POV makes your writing sharper, more focused, and more powerful. The assignment may or may not tell you which POV to use. So, already knowing when to shift or avoid the wrong one is setting yourself up to earn your bonus.

W.R.I.T.E. R.I.C.H.™

## CHALLENGE YOURSELF

1. Take three common writing prompts and rewrite your opening sentence in 1st, 2nd, and 3rd person to see how the tone changes.
2. Choose the one that fits best.

## SELF-CHECK

- Did I match my POV to the assignment?
- Did I avoid including the reader unless I was supposed to?
- Did I sound like a reliable, thoughtful writer?

## FINANCIAL ADVICE

Write like someone who knows the rules. It will surprise some grown-ups that you know such a game-changing skill. When other students are casually dropping "we" and "you" all over their essays, your 3rd-person structure will feel like money in the bank.

# NEXT UP

Your skills are rich. Your habits are strong. Your leadership is showing. WRITE RICH Legacy Moves™ is the next chapter. Let's explore how to turn these tips you've learned into a lasting impact through public writing, passion projects, and even published pieces. It's time to leave your writing fingerprint on the world. Let's go.

W.R.I.T.E. R.I.C.H.™

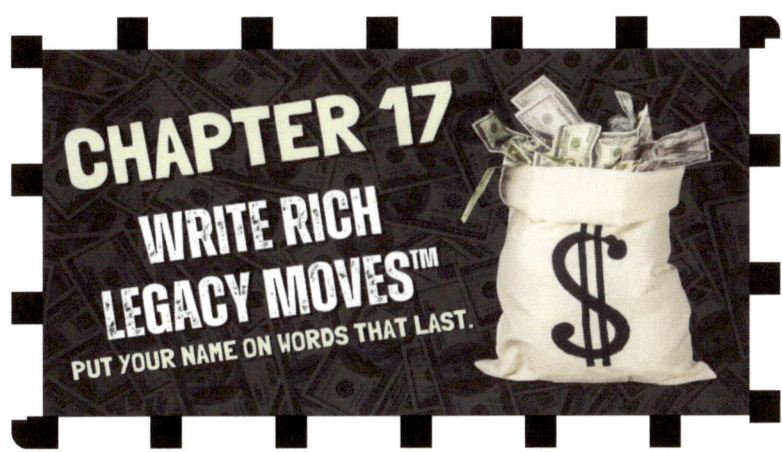

## BRIEF EXPLANATION

You've built skill. You've built confidence. You've even built leadership. But now it's time to create an impact bigger than grades or points. Your writing can be an enduring mark that outlives the class bell: your legacy. Your words can live on outside the classroom. They can inspire others, shift the culture, spark a movement, or change how someone sees the world.

In the real world, people write to:
- Start podcasts
- Launch blogs
- Publish books
- Create spoken word videos
- Write for the school paper
- Post captions that matter
- Drop college essays that change everything

That's what WRITE RICH Legacy Moves™ are all about taking every skill you've learned and using your abilities to benefit you. Something that earns you respect, builds your resume, and leaves a mark long after you're gone. This chapter will show you how to move like a writer who's not just turning in assignments, but turning words into a legacy.

## STORY TIME

### *Aaliyah's Poem That Hit the City*

Aaliyah (8th grade) wrote a poem in her journal about how it felt to be followed in a store because of how she looked. She never meant for anyone to read it. But her teacher asked to share it during a school assembly. The crowd went silent. Some students teared up. A local organizer asked to reprint it in a youth magazine. That one piece turned into a

published poem, an invite to speak at a youth conference, and a scholarship opportunity.

Aaliyah didn't chase fame. She told her truth. And her writing became part of something bigger.

**W.R.I.T.E. R.I.C.H.™**

# REAL TALK & HOW TO

*The L.E.G.A.C.Y.™ Blueprint: Turning Skill Into Impact*

| Steps | What it means | Money Move | Writing Move |
|---|---|---|---|
| **L**aunch a Project | Start a new stream of income | Start a new stream of income | Choose a cause, story, or topic that matters to you and launch something: blog, zine, YouTube, or school initiative. |
| **E**levate a Voice | Use your platform to give someone else value | Add value to someone else's brand | Interview, highlight, or uplift others in your writing (e.g., your grandma, classmate, or neighborhood hero). |

W.R.I.T.E. R.I.C.H.™

| **G**et It Out There | Money in a safe can't grow | Circulate your currency | Submit to contests, post your edited work, or share at open mics or community events. |
|---|---|---|---|
| **A**rchive Your Wins | Track your earnings | Keep record of your profits | Save your best work: essays, poems, letters, or feedback. Build your writing portfolio. |
| **C**onnect With Purpose | Build writing relationships | Build your financial network | Find mentors, join writing circles, collaborate, and get feedback. |
| **Y**ield Influence | Let your writing earn on its own | Compound your influence | Use your work to teach, inspire younger kids, or shift thinking on |

| | | | important issues. |
|---|---|---|---|
| | | | |

> 💡 **Pro Tip:**
> Legacy writing doesn't have to be perfect. It just has to be true, focused, and ready to be seen.

## THE SKILL THAT PAYS

- Visibility: Strong writing in public spaces leads to opportunities, especially for teens who speak up.
- Influence: You help shape conversations, shift opinions, and make change.
- Resume Builder: Colleges, jobs, and programs want students with real-world projects and published work.
- Purpose: Your writing becomes more than homework; it becomes a mission.

## CHALLENGE YOURSELF

1. Choose one Legacy Move this month:
    a. Submit your best poem or essay to a contest or youth magazine.
    b. Start a Google Doc portfolio of your best writing and share it with a mentor.
    c. Write a letter to the editor, post a blog or Medium article, or start a passion page.
    d. Share something powerful at your next school event or talent show.

**Bonus:** Partner with a peer and elevate someone else's story. Help them find their voice while you use yours.

## SELF-CHECK

- Is there a message I've written that could help someone else?
- What piece of writing am I most proud of and where could I share it?
- Have I saved and organized my strongest work?
- Am I leaving behind work that represents my voice, story, and strength?

## FINANCIAL ADVICE

Wealth is bigger than money. It brings impact. You can build something that earns attention, trust, and change. Your words are assets. Don't bury them. Release them. Grow them. Leave them behind to speak for you.

## NEXT UP

This could be the end of the series or it could be the beginning of your writing empire. Either way, the next move is yours. W.R.I.T.E. R.I.C.H.™ was never just a bunch of lessons for my Ohio students. It has always been a wealth-building, life changing mindset. So, now, what will you do with your writing fortune? Will you teach others? Will you publish? Will you lead? Will you change your city, your school, your family, or just your own self-worth?

W.R.I.T.E. R.I.C.H.™

## *Dear Soon-to-be-Rich Writer,*

From 1996 to 2023, there was no artificial intelligence (AI) in my classroom or office. Just me, my chalk or marker, and a stubborn heart full of determination to equip students from tough neighborhoods with the skills and confidence to become therapists, chefs, nurses, executives, soldiers, teachers, principals, authors, pharmacists, managers, business owners, doctors, lawyers, cosmetologists, psychologists, police officers, and so much more. I wanted them to leave me in the dust! In case you haven't noticed, it's rough out here in these streets. Many of my students' writing skills weren't where they needed to be to pass me up. So what! I refused to let any gaps limit what we could achieve.

    I just did what needed to be done the old-school way. Long, handwritten lesson plans and lots of red pens were my best friends. We tackled writing assignments that left my students with hand cramps. We had tougher talks that left some of them (and some parents) hating my guts. So what! I spent nights, weekends, and holidays grading until the sun came up or answering questions about assignments. Google Classroom gave me twenty-four/seven access to every student. I was in HEAVEN! Most days, I was hit with complaints or every excuse in the book, but I pushed through. I saw life-changing greatness behind their resistance.

My students' success stories didn't come from shortcuts. They came from skill-building, mindset shifts, high expectations, fussing at me, and relentless encouragement. Before you let AI help you write, you'll need to know the basics yourself. You don't have to enjoy writing to be good at it. If you don't understand how

writing should work for you, AI can't fix it. You won't know how to correct AI. Using AI without having writing skills is like giving your money to a stranger and hoping you can use whatever the stranger buys for you. You give up control. Without strong skills, you'll always need AI. If AI does all your thinking, one day it could **replace** you instead of helping you get paid. Easy isn't always good.

That's why this book helps you build your own writing skills first. You should be the one in charge.

When it came time to create this workbook, I didn't need AI to write it for me. My legacy gave me more than enough content. I used AI as my assistant and not my author. I dictated the direction, my methods, the stories, the voice, every correction, etc. AI just helped me organize and refine my ideas faster. It's a great tool that can help you be more efficient. But artificial intelligence couldn't give me the wisdom I've earned from decades of doing this work face-to-face with students.

W.R.I.T.E. R.I.C.H.™ is my love letter for every single student who deserves or needs tools that speak their language, respect their reality, and remind them that writing can be a key to their dreams. I've never just taught how to write paragraphs; I taught and still teach how to build power,  purpose, and possibility… one word at a time.

Cheering for You,
Bridget Lambright-Tommelleo, M.Ed.

W.R.I.T.E. R.I.C.H.™

## 🎯 My Plans Before My Paycheck: *From Now to Wow*

*Stack your days, build a life that pays.*

### 🔑 Today

My name is:
_____
_____

I am _____ years old

I live in:
_____
_____
(City, State)

My hobbies are:
_____
_____

My happy colors are:
_____
_____

My happy place is:
_____
_____

Because:
_____
_____
_____

W.R.I.T.E. R.I.C.H.™

I will be 26 in _____ years

## ⌛ By the time I'm 26...

I will earn $_____ per hour

I will live in: _____
(City, State)

My home will be: ☐ Apartment ☐ Condo ☐ House ☐ Other _____

My hobbies will include:
_____
_____
_____

I will drive a:
_____
_____
_____

I will have graduated from:
_____
(College/Trade School/Other)

My career or business will be:
_____

I will work for:
☐ Myself
☐ A company
☐ A school
☐ Other _____

**W.R.I.T.E. R.I.C.H.™**

My job will help people by:
_____
_____

I will dress mostly in:
_____
(colors, style)

The kind of people I'll spend time with:
_____
_____

I will be proud of myself for:
_____
_____

## ⟳ Planning My Future

1. To get there, what do I need to do after high school?
(College? Military? Trade School? Business Start-Up? Apprenticeship?)




2. To get into that, what do I need to do in middle and/or high school?
(Grades, activities, skills, mentality, etc.)

W.R.I.T.E. R.I.C.H.™

3. To prepare for #2's answer, what can I start doing now? (Classes, clubs, reading, mentors, choices, etc.)



4. What habits do I need to build today to match my future self?

- ☐ Waking up earlier
- ☐ Doing homework
- ☐ Refusing to give up on myself
- ☐ Being kinder
- ☐ Saving money
- ☐ Staying focused during class
- ☐ Other:

## 🔍 Reality Check Reflection

One choice I'm making now that helps my future:
_____
_____

One choice I'm making now that could hurt my future:
_____
_____

One adult I know who lives the kind of life I want:
_____
_____

One question about their success I'd ask them if I could:
_____
_____

W.R.I.T.E. R.I.C.H.™

My current weakness I want to work on is:
_____
_____

The goal I'm most excited about achieving is:
_____
_____

I am so excited about achieving this goal because:
_____
_____

## 💰 WRITE RICH™ BONUS

What skills do I need to make my dreams pay off like money?


How can writing help me get to the life I want?


My notes for myself:

# W.R.I.T.E. R.I.C.H.™ Vocabulary Bank

| $2-$5 Words | $10-$20 Upgrade | $50 Upgrade | $100 Rich |
|---|---|---|---|
| Nothing, something, anything, everything, thing | Be specific | Elaborate | Be precise |
| big | large, tall | enormous, hefty | colossal, mammoth, gigantic |
| small | little, tiny | slight, modest | minuscule, microscopic |
| good | fine, nice | great, worthy | exceptional, outstanding |
| bad | mean, poor | terrible, awful | atrocious, appalling, abominable |
| happy | glad, cheerful | excited, joyful | elated, jubilant, euphoric |
| sad | upset, gloomy | miserable, heartbroken | despondent, devastated |
| fast | quick, speedy | swift, brisk | rapid, lightning-fast |
| slow | sluggish, steady | gradual, delayed | unhurried, leisurely |
| smart | clever, bright | intelligent, sharp | brilliant, genius-level |
| dumb | clueless, slow | dull, simple | ignorant, uninformed |

# W.R.I.T.E. R.I.C.H.™ Vocabulary Bank

| $2-$5 Words | $10-$20 Upgrade | $50 Upgrade | $100 Rich |
|---|---|---|---|
| like | enjoy, prefer | admire, value | appreciate, cherish |
| hate | dislike, avoid | despise, loathe | detest, abhor |
| talk | say, chat | explain, discuss | articulate, express clearly |
| walk | move, stroll | march, stride | saunter, meander, trek |
| funny | silly, goofy | entertaining, comical | hilarious, side-splitting |
| mad | angry, annoyed | frustrated, furious | enraged, livid, outraged |
| nice | kind, friendly | thoughtful, warm | compassionate, gracious |
| mean | rude, cold | harsh, unfair | malicious, spiteful |
| pretty | cute, lovely | beautiful, stunning | radiant, breathtaking |
| ugly | plain, odd | unattractive, rough | hideous, repulsive |
| scary | creepy, eerie | frightening, shocking | terrifying, horrifying |
| cool | neat, trendy | interesting, stylish | impressive, captivating |
| hot | warm, toasty | boiling, steaming | scorching, sweltering |
| cold | chilly, icy | freezing, frosty | arctic, bone-chilling |

## *W.R.I.T.E. R.I.C.H.™ Vocabulary Bank*

| $2-$5 Words | $10-$20 Upgrade | $50 Upgrade | $100 Rich |
|---|---|---|---|
| tired | sleepy, worn-out | exhausted, drained | depleted, fatigued |
| big deal | okay, fair | important, major | life-changing, pivotal |
| try | attempt, test | practice, experiment | persevere, pursue |
| work | job, task | effort, labour | Mission, grind, hustle |
| scared | nervous, anxious | shaken, uneasy | petrified, terrified |
| look | glance, see | notice, observe | examine, scrutinize |
| see | notice, view | spot, observe | perceive, detect |
| weird | odd, strange | unusual, awkward | bizarre, peculiar |
| fine | okay, alright | decent, satisfying | excellent, superior |
| loud | noisy, rowdy | blaring, booming | thunderous, deafening |
| quiet | soft, still | hushed, peaceful | silent, tranquil |
| love | like, care for | admire, adore | treasure, worship |
| bored | dull, uninterested | restless, sleepy | disengaged, apathetic |
| clean | neat, tidy | spotless, polished | immaculate, pristine |
| dirty | messy, gross | grimy, stained | filthy, contaminated |

# *W.R.I.T.E. R.I.C.H.™ Vocabulary Bank*

| $2-$5 Words | $10-$20 Upgrade | $50 Upgrade | $100 Rich |
|---|---|---|---|
| eat | munch, snack | consume, devour | feast, inhale |
| run | jog, dash | race, sprint | bolt, charge |
| fight | argue, yell | battle, clash | conflict, war |
| help | aid, assist | support, guide | advocate, empower |
| stop | pause, quit | freeze, cease | terminate, abandon |
| begin | start, open | launch, commence | initiate, inaugurate |
| end | stop, close | finish, conclude | terminate, wrap up |
| build | make, form | create, design | construct, engineer |
| think | guess, figure | wonder, consider | analyze, brainstorm |
| learn | study, review | understand, grasp | master, internalize |

## Chapter 2 Review: The B.U.D.G.E.T. Method™

**Directions:**

**Fill in the missing boxes. Reflect on how to apply your answers to your writing. Go back to the chapter to help your memory. Write your own Money Move to explain how you'll apply the method in your writing.**

**Name:** _____

**Date:** _____

| Letter (Step) | What The Letter Stands For | What it Means in Writing | Visual | Your Money Move |
|---|---|---|---|---|
| | | What are your topic ideas? What's your big idea and where can it go? | 💡 | |
| | | What's the one message or purpose that connects everything in your writing? | ⭕ | |
| | | How will you break your big idea into smaller, organized | ✂ | |

# W.R.I.T.E. R.I.C.H.™

| | | | | |
|---|---|---|---|---|
| | | parts or paragraphs? | | |
| | | How will you stay on topic and avoid distractions or off-topic thoughts? | | |
| | | How will you stretch your thinking with examples, explanations, and evidence? | | |
| | | How will you check your work, count your sentences, or review for completion and focus? | | |

W.R.I.T.E. R.I.C.H.™

## Chapter 3 Review: The B.I.L.L.$.™ Sentence Stack

**Directions:**

Fill in the missing boxes. Reflect on how to apply your answers to your writing. Go back to the chapter to help your memory. Write your own Money Move to explain how you'll apply the method in your writing.

Name: _____

Date: _____

| Letter (Step) | What The Letter Stands For | What it Means in Writing | Visual | Your Money Move |
|---|---|---|---|---|
| | | Pause at natural breaks. | | |
| | | Find one idea per sentence. | | |
| | | Connect ideas the right way. | | |
| | | Keep sentences wallet sized. | | |
| | | Swap weak verbs/words. | | |

W.R.I.T.E. R.I.C.H.™

## Chapter 4 Review: The W.O.R.T.H.™ System

**Directions:**

Fill in the missing boxes. Reflect on how to apply your answers to your writing. Go back to the chapter to help your memory. Write your own Money Move to explain how you'll apply the method in your writing.

Name: _____

Date: _____

| Letter (Step) | What The Letter Stands For | What it Means in Writing | Visual | Your Money Move |
|---|---|---|---|---|
| | | _____ Out for Weak Words – "good," "bad," "stuff," "thing," "nice," etc. | 🚫 | |
| | | _____ a Word Bank, collect high-value words from music, books, and convo. | 📚 | |
| | | _____ a word's value, ask: Does this word paint a picture or | 🎨 | |

125

| | | leave it blank? | | |
|---|---|---|---|---|
| | | _____ the tone, pick words that match the vibe you're aiming for. | 🎯 | |
| | | _____ with verbs, verbs are action money and they move the reader. | 🏃 | |

## Chapter 5 Review: H.O.O.K.$. Formula™

**Directions:**

Fill in the missing boxes. Reflect on how to apply your answers to your writing. Go back to the chapter to help your memory. Write your own Money Move to explain how you'll apply the method in your writing.

Name: _____

Date: _____

| Letter (Step) | What The Letter Stands For | What it Means in Writing | Visual | Your Money Move |
|---|---|---|---|---|
| | | _____ the heat, start with something bold, dramatic, or urgent. | 🔥 | |
| | | _____ a big idea, not a question, blow your reader's mind. | 💡 | |
| | | _____ the emotion and tap into feelings: curiosity, anger, pride, humor. | ♡ | |

|  |  | ___ titles short & sharp; make it tight and punchy |  |  |
|  |  | ___ it like a brand and make it catchy, clever, and unforgettable. |  |  |

# Chapter 6 Review: The R.E.C.E.I.P.T.™ Formula

**Directions:**

Fill in the missing boxes. Reflect on how to apply your answers to your writing. Go back to the chapter to help your memory. Write your own Money Move to explain how you'll apply the method in your writing.

Name: _____

Date: _____

| Letter (Step) | What The Letter Stands For | What it Means in Writing | Visual | Your Money Move |
|---|---|---|---|---|
| | | Tell a real or believable situation, use a moment from your life, a story, or a common situation your reader will connect with. | | |
| | | Give a fact, stat, quote, or source. Add information that shows your idea is legit. | | |
| | | Link the example to your main point, explain | | |

129

# W.R.I.T.E. R.I.C.H.™

|  |  | how the story proves what you're saying. |  |  |
|---|---|---|---|---|
|  |  | Break it down in your own words, don't assume the reader gets it; spell it out. | 💬 |  |
|  |  | Add names, time, setting, and feelings, be specific about who, where, when, what, why, and how. | 📋 |  |
|  |  | Help the reader visualize it, use sensory language: how did it feel, smell, sound? | 🎨 |  |
|  |  | Bring it home to your main idea, end the paragraph by clearly stating what we should believe now. | 👜 |  |

# Chapter 7 Review: The R.E.C.E.I.P.T.S.™ Guide

**Directions:**

Fill in the missing boxes. Reflect on how to apply your answers to your writing. Go back to the chapter to help your memory. Write your own Money Move to explain how you'll apply the method in your writing.

Name: _____

Date: _____

| Letter (Step) | What The Letter Stands For | What it Means in Writing | Visual | Your Money Move |
|---|---|---|---|---|
| | | Ends a full thought | | |
| | | Pauses and separates | | |
| | | Shows you're asking | | |
| | | Adds emotion or energy | | |
| | | Shows what someone said | | |
| | | Add extra info quietly | | |
| | | Introduce or separate related items | | |
| | | Show ownership or missing letters | | |

# Chapter 8 Review: The C.A.S.H.™ Blueprint

**Directions:**

Fill in the missing boxes. Reflect on how to apply your answers to your writing. Go back to the chapter to help your memory. Write your own Money Move to explain how you'll apply the method in your writing.

Name: _____

Date: _____

| Letter (Step) | What The Letter Stands For | What it Means in Writing | Visual | Your Money Move |
|---|---|---|---|---|
| | | One clear sentence stating your main point | | |
| | | 1–2 sentences of evidence, examples, or reasons | | |
| | | 3-4 sentences explaining how or why your evidence matters | | |
| | | 2–3 sentences tying | | |

| | | everything back to your Claim + leaving the reader thinking or convinced | | |

W.R.I.T.E. R.I.C.H.™

## Chapter 8 Review: The D.E.P.O.S.I.T™ Blueprint

**Directions:**

**Fill in the missing boxes. Reflect on how to apply your answers to your writing. Go back to the chapter to help your memory. Write your own Money Move to explain how you'll apply the method in your writing.**

**Name:** _____

**Date:** _____

| Letter (Step) | What The Letter Stands For | What it Means in Writing | Visual | Your Money Move |
|---|---|---|---|---|
| | | Write a clear topic sentence that tells readers what the paragraph is about. | 💬 | |
| | | Clarify what your topic means and why it matters. | 🧠 | |
| | | Use examples, facts, quotes, or observations that support your point. | 📄 | |

**W.R.I.T.E. R.I.C.H.™**

| | | | Describe how your evidence connects to your claim. | | |
|---|---|---|---|---|---|
| | | | Add another example or reason to deepen the argument. | | |
| | | | Use words or phrases to link ideas clearly. | | |
| | | | End with a sentence that restates or reinforces the main idea. | | |

W.R.I.T.E. R.I.C.H.™

## Chapter 9 Review: The P.A.I.D.™ Strategy

**Directions:**

Fill in the missing boxes. Reflect on how to apply your answers to your writing. Go back to the chapter to help your memory. Write your own Money Move to explain how you'll apply the method in your writing.

Name: _____

Date: _____

| Letter (Step) | What The Letter Stands For | What it Means in Writing | Visual | Your Money Move |
|---|---|---|---|---|
| | | Use an outline, know how many paragraphs you need and what each one's job is. | | |
| | | Make sure each paragraph supports the same main idea or claim. | | |
| | | Use transition words/phrases to connect ideas smoothly. | | |
| | | Restate your main idea in a | | |

|  |  | fresh way and leave a lasting thought or call to action. |  |  |

# Bonus Chapter Review: W.R.I.T.E. R.I.C.H.™ Investment Plan

**Directions:**

Fill in the missing boxes. Reflect on how to apply your answers to your writing. Go back to the chapter to help your memory. Write your own Money Move to explain how you'll apply the method in your writing.

Name: _____

Date: _____

| Letter (Step) | What The Letter Stands For | What it Means in Writing | Visual | Your Money Move |
|---|---|---|---|---|
| | | Use precise, meaningful vocabulary. | | |
| | | Structure, grammar, and punctuation matter. | | |
| | | Create strong claims, themes, or thesis statements. | | |
| | | Use examples, explanations, and logic. | | |
| | | Revise and polish every draft. | | |

# W.R.I.T.E. R.I.C.H.™

|  |  | Pay attention to mentor texts, directions, and examples. | 📖 |  |
|--|--|--|--|--|
|  |  | Always back up your ideas with evidence and details. | 📁 |  |
|  |  | Know who you are writing to and why. | 🎯 |  |
|  |  | Put your best foot forward from beginning to end. | 💼 |  |

# Chapter 10 Review: F.L.A.V.O.R.™ Style Voice Moves

**Directions:**

Fill in the missing boxes. Reflect on how to apply your answers to your writing. Go back to the chapter to help your memory. Write your own Money Move to explain how you'll apply the method in your writing.

Name: _____

Date: _____

| Letter (Step) | What The Letter Stands For | What it Means in Writing | Visual | Your Money Move |
|---|---|---|---|---|
| | | Are you serious, funny, emotional, or bold? Pick the tone that fits your purpose. | | |
| | | Swap plain words for vivid ones that match your message (see Vocabulary Bank). | | |
| | | Share your slang, experience, or a little humor without losing clarity. | | |

| | | | | |
|---|---|---|---|---|
| | | Short, punchy lines + longer expressive ones = rhythm. | 📏 | |
| | | Break a rule on purpose, not by accident, and know the difference, | 📐 | |
| | | If it sounds boring or fake, rewrite it until it feels like you. | 🔊 | |

# Chapter 11 Review: The C.R.E.D.I.T.™ Checklist

**Directions:**

Fill in the missing boxes. Reflect on how to apply your answers to your writing. Go back to the chapter to help your memory. Write your own Money Move to explain how you'll apply the method in your writing.

Name: _____

Date: _____

| Letter (Step) | What The Letter Stands For | What it Means in Writing | Visual | Your Money Move |
|---|---|---|---|---|
| | | Respect your title like a paycheck stub. | | |
| | | Separate bills correctly. | | |
| | | Spell check is like counterfeit detection. | | |
| | | Accurate billing matters. | | |
| | | Use one consistent currency. | | |
| | | Neatness = value. | | |

## Chapter 12 Review: The H.U.S.T.L.E.™ Method

**Directions:**

Fill in the missing boxes. Reflect on how to apply your answers to your writing. Go back to the chapter to help your memory. Write your own Money Move to explain how you'll apply the method in your writing.

Name: _____

Date: _____

| Letter (Step) | What The Letter Stands For | What it Means in Writing | Visual | Your Money Move |
|---|---|---|---|---|
| | | Start by showing your strengths, skills, or personal story. | | |
| | | Think: 'Who's reading this? What do they care about?' | | |
| | | Use examples, facts, or past wins to support your message. | | |
| | | Avoid weak language like 'I think,' 'maybe.' | | |
| | | Use C.A.S.H.™ or full essay | | |

143

W.R.I.T.E. R.I.C.H.™

|  |  | layout to stay focused. |  |  |
|---|---|---|---|---|
|  |  | End with a call to action or bold takeaway. | ←<br>END |  |

# Chapter 13 Review: The P.A.Y. D.A.Y.™ Prompt Decoder

**Directions:**

**Fill in the missing boxes. Reflect on how to apply your answers to your writing. Go back to the chapter to help your memory. Write your own Money Move to explain how you'll apply the method in your writing.**

Name: _____

Date: _____

| Letter (Step) | What The Letter Stands For | What it Means in Writing | Visual | Your Money Move |
|---|---|---|---|---|
| | | Pay Attention to the Prompt. Read the contract before the deal. | | |
| | | Ask: What is it really asking me to do? Rephrase the prompt in your own words to aim your answer right. | | |
| | | You don't get paid without a plan. Decide your main | | |

145

# W.R.I.T.E. R.I.C.H.™

| | | | | |
|---|---|---|---|---|
| | | point and supporting evidence. | | |
| | | Choose the right voice for the job. Use 1st, 2nd, or 3rd person based on the prompt. | 🎤 | |
| | | Don't leave money on the table. Some prompts have two or more parts. | ✓ | |
| | | Receipts get respect. Use details, quotes, examples, whatever backs you up. | 📄 | |

# Chapter 14 Review: The W.E.A.L.T.H.™ Routine

**Directions:**

**Fill in the missing boxes. Reflect on how to apply your answers to your writing. Go back to the chapter to help your memory. Write your own Money Move to explain how you'll apply the method in your writing.**

Name: _____

Date: _____

| Letter (Step) | What The Letter Stands For | What it Means in Writing | Visual | Your Money Move |
|---|---|---|---|---|
| | | Spend 5–10 minutes a day writing: journal, captions, prompts, or story ideas. | | |
| | | Choose an old paragraph and apply the C.R.E.D.I.T.™ method weekly. | | |
| | | Read songs, blogs, or essays and ask: "Why does this hit?" | | |
| | | Add 5–10 new words to your personal Vocabulary Bank each week. | | |

| | | Save old writing samples and compare monthly to see progress. | | |
|---|---|---|---|---|
| | | Edit a friend's paragraph or teach them a tip you've learned. | | |

# W.R.I.T.E. R.I.C.H.™

## Chapter 15 Review: The G.I.V.E.™ Method

**Directions:**

Fill in the missing boxes. Reflect on how to apply your answers to your writing. Go back to the chapter to help your memory. Write your own Money Move to explain how you'll apply the method in your writing.

Name: _____

Date: _____

| Letter (Step) | What The Letter Stands For | What it Means in Writing | Visual | Your Money Move |
|---|---|---|---|---|
| | | Say: "Want me to help break it down?" instead of "Just copy me." | | |
| | | Ask before you act "What part's confusing you?" | | |
| | | Celebrate wins like: "That example hit!" or "You fixed your run-ons, let's go!" | | |
| | | Walk them through fixes using B.U.D.G.E.T.™, C.A.S.H.™, etc. | | |

149

# W.R.I.T.E. R.I.C.H.™

## Chapter 16 Review: Person Pays

**Directions:**

**Fill in the missing boxes. Reflect on how to apply your answers to your writing. Go back to the chapter to help your memory. Write your own Money Move to explain how you'll apply the method in your writing.**

**Name:** _____

**Date:** _____

| Letter (Step) | What The Letter Stands For | What it Means in Writing | Visual | Your Money Move |
|---|---|---|---|---|
| | | Pick the right person, just like choosing the right bank account for your money | 🎯 | |
| | | Know the reason you're writing: Is it personal (1st), instructional (2nd), or informational/storytelling (3rd)? | 📌 | |
| | | Pick the person that speaks clearly to your reader: "I" for personal, "you" for direct, "they" for | 🗣️ | |

|  |  | distant and professional. |  |  |

W.R.I.T.E. R.I.C.H.™

## Chapter 17 Review: The L.E.G.A.C.Y.™ Blueprint

**Directions:**

Fill in the missing boxes. Reflect on how to apply your answers to your writing. Go back to the chapter to help your memory. Write your own Money Move to explain how you'll apply the method in your writing.

Name: _____

Date: _____

| Letter (Step) | What The Letter Stands For | What it Means in Writing | Visual | Your Money Move |
|---|---|---|---|---|
| | | Choose a cause, story, or topic that matters to you and launch something: blog, zine, YouTube, or school initiative. | 🚀 | |
| | | Interview, highlight, or uplift others in your writing (e.g., your grandma, classmate, or neighborhood hero). | 📢 | |

W.R.I.T.E. R.I.C.H.™

|  |  | Submit to contests, post your edited work, or share at open mics and community events. | 🌍 |  |
|--|--|--|--|--|
|  |  | Save your best work: essays, poems, letters, or feedback. | 📁 |  |
|  |  | Find mentors, join writing circles, collaborate, and get feedback. | 🤝 |  |
|  |  | Use your work to teach, inspire younger kids. | 💡 |  |

## *Special Thanks*

To my husband, Andy, for proving to me that when it's the right one, two is better than one. You have lightened my load more than I could have imagined.

To my children, you both are amazing adults and I thank God for choosing to give you both to me. B1: You're the best thing that ever happened to me & B2: The point of it all is I love you.

To (most of) my former students, I'm struggling for the best words to express my deepest appreciation. You completely changed me. You chipped away at my privilege and judgment. You humbled me. You're my legacy. My life has been a dream and full of surprise blessings because of you. Now, let me go dry my tears!

## About the Author

Ms. Lambright (Ms. LT) is *that* teacher.

The one who made sure that even kids from the toughest neighborhoods or circumstances had the skills and confidence to become doctors, lawyers, authors, entrepreneurs, nurses, accountants, chefs, police officers, therapists, educators, cosmetologists, engineers, military leaders, executives, community leaders, and more. Now, their children are thriving too. With 30 years of experience as a teacher, principal, mentor, trainer, "school mom," business owner, and district leader, Ms. LT is a force for transformation. She's taught English, trained teachers, coached single moms, and helped over a thousand students crush self-doubt and unlock their full potential.

Her bold approach has earned her national recognition, including the prestigious Stephen Sondheim Inspirational Teacher Award from The John F. Kennedy Center for the Performing Arts and a Secretary of State Commendation.

Oh, and yes, she's Googleable.

www.ingramcontent.com/pod-product-compliance
Lightning Source LLC
Chambersburg PA
CBHW042346300426
44110CB00032B/44